TELLING SOMEONE WHERE TO GO

EQUALS INVESTIGATIONS

GROWTH PATTERNS

A Middle-school Mathematics Unit Focusing on Linear and Exponential Growth Functions

Lawrence Hall of Science
University of California at Berkeley

EQUALS INVESTIGATIONS

REMOTE RULERS

A Middle-school Mathematics Unit Focusing on the Relationship Between Algebraic Graphs and Graphs From Real Data Involving Direct and Inverse Variation

Lawrence Hall of Science
University of California at Berkeley

EQUALS INVESTIGATIONS

TELLING SOMEONE WHERE TO GO

A Middle-school Mathematics Unit Focusing on Measurement of Distance and Angle

Lawrence Hall of Science
University of California at Berkeley

EQUALS INVESTIGATIONS

FLEA-SIZED SURGEONS

A Middle-school Mathematics Unit Focusing on Surface Area, Volume, and Scale

Lawrence Hall of Science
University of California at Berkeley

EQUALS INVESTIGATIONS

SCATTER MATTERS

A Middle-school Mathematics Unit Focusing on Scatterplots, Correlation, and Cause and Effect

Lawrence Hall of Science
University of California at Berkeley

EQUALS INVESTIGATIONS

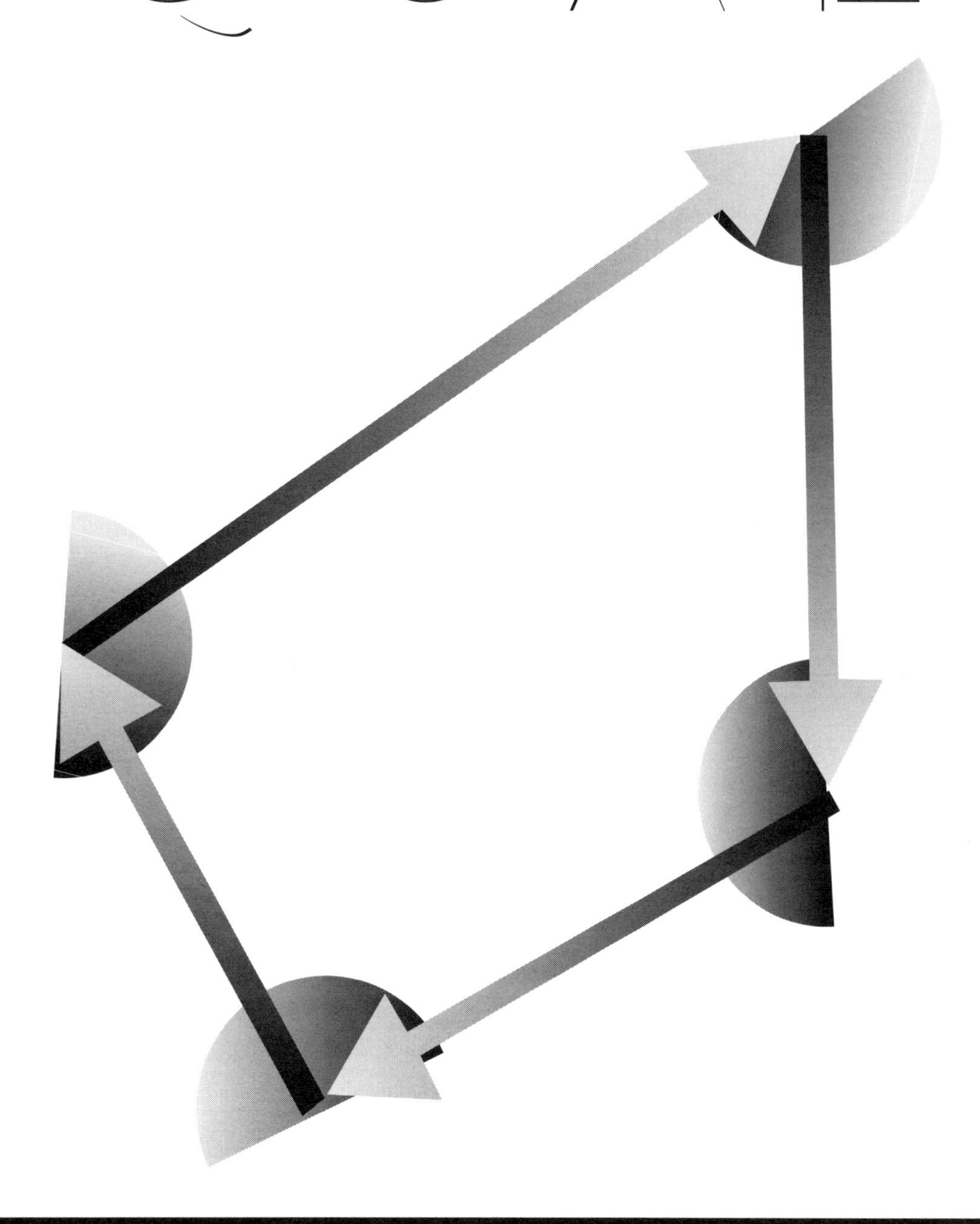

TELLING SOMEONE WHERE TO GO

A MIDDLE-SCHOOL MATHEMATICS UNIT FOCUSING ON MEASUREMENT OF DISTANCE AND ANGLE

LAWRENCE HALL OF SCIENCE
UNIVERSITY OF CALIFORNIA AT BERKELEY

The Lawrence Hall of Science is a public science center, teacher inservice institution, and research unit in science and mathematics education at the University of California at Berkeley. For many years, it has developed curricula and teaching strategies to improve mathematics, science, and computer education at all levels, and to increase public understanding of those areas.

For information and additional copies, contact:

EQUALS
Lawrence Hall of Science
University of California
Berkeley, CA 94720

attn: Investigations Units

Printed in the United States of America.

Design & illustration by Seventeenth Street Studios

Work on the Investigations Units was supported by the National Science Foundation under grant number MDR-8850720.

Printing (last digit): 9 8 7 6 5 4 3 2 1

ISBN 0-912511-59-1

Contents

Preface

The *Investigations Units,* including *Telling Someone Where To Go,* are published by the EQUALS program at the Lawrence Hall of Science, University of California at Berkeley.

EQUALS is a teacher education program that since 1977 has helped elementary and secondary educators acquire methods and materials to attract minority and female students to mathematics. The EQUALS program supports a problem-solving approach to mathematics, including having students working in groups, using active assessment methods, and incorporating a broad mathematics curriculum presented to students in a variety of contexts.

We are pleased to present the *Investigations Units,* which were developed by the *Investigations Mathematics Curriculum Project* from January 1990 to January 1993 at the Office of the President of the University of California. The project was supported by funding from the National Science Foundation and led by Dr. Elizabeth Stage, Principal Investigator. Dan Brutlag was Project Coordinator and primary author, Richard Stanley, Professional Development Project, University of California Berkeley, was a contributing author, and Phil Daro, Executive Director of the California Mathematics Project (1990-92) and Director of Mathematics for the New Standards Project (1992-present) was the primary advisor to the project. Jan Dougall and Evy McPherson served as the Teacher Coordinator, and Publications Coordinator respectively.

The Advisory Committee consisted of the following: James Caballero and Philip Curtis, UCLA; Jeremy Kilpatrick, University of Georgia; Alfred Manaster, University of California, San Diego; Tej Pandey, California Department of Education; Thomas Romberg, University of Wisconsin; and Judah Schwartz, Harvard University. Other contributors were Ruth Cossey, Mills College; José Gutierrez, San Francisco State University; and Sharon Ross, California State University at Chico.

Revisions were made based on the suggestions and ideas from Ada Wada, Berkeley; Carole Maples, Walnut Creek; Donna Luporini and Jesse Ragent, Berkeley; Carlos Cabana and Philip Tucher, San Lorenzo; and Linda Lutjens, Hayward.

Final editing for publication was undertaken by EQUALS beginning in April 1993. We would like to thank the following editorial reviewers who took drafts on the plane, translated student pages on vacation, and basically placed many other responsibilities on hold to publish the units. We couldn't have done it without you! Thanks to Terri Belcher, Grace Dávila Coates, José Franco, Kay Gilliland, Nancy Kreinberg, and Jean Kerr Stenmark.

Principal editing and coordination responsibilities were shared by Karen Mayfield and Bob Whitlow; copy editing was managed by Kay Gilliland. Student pages were diligently translated by Laura López, Deborah Martínez, and Patricia Zuno, with José Franco and Grace Dávila Coates coordinating. Other assistance was provided by Kathryn Baston, Bob Capune, Miguel Casillas, Alison DeLorenzo, Carol Gray, Ellen Humm, Louise Lang, Gen Llamas, Linda Morgan, Virginia Thompson, and Helen Raymond.

We also thank the many teachers who have tried out the *Investigations* materials while they were being developed and edited. We appreciate their feedback and their willingness to try a new approach to mathematics instruction.

We hope you and your students will enjoy the *Investigations Units* and will find that they make a real contribution to your mathematics program.

—Karen Mayfield
—Bob Whitlow

Berkeley, California, September, 1994

Notes

■ FULL ACCESS FOR EVERY STUDENT

Imagine a classroom where middle school students are working in groups of four or five, comparing notes and helping each other complete the task they have been working on for a week. There is a busy hum as the teacher circulates to respond to questions and requests. Although the class includes students from all "achievement" levels, it is impossible to tell which are "high achievers" and which are not. All are actively engaged in the work at hand.

The EQUALS programs, along with other educators, have a vision of full access to learning for every student.

Mathematics education requires new models. The 1992 *Mathematics Framework for California Public Schools* and the 1989 National Council of Teachers of Mathematics *Curriculum and Evaluation Standards for School Mathematics* both advocate a problem-based curriculum with more depth than traditional exercises. We need to give students sustained work that involves higher levels of thinking, planning their own strategies, and communicating their ideas.

The *Investigations Units,* a set of five units authored by Dan Brutlag at the University of California, are published by the EQUALS programs to contribute to this vision for middle school.

■ WHAT'S IN THESE NOTES?

These notes cannot replace an inservice session with someone who has taught the units, which you should attend. Meanwhile, here are some helpful ideas about groupwork, language issues, assessment, grades, manipulatives, and calculators—all essential for the units to contribute to that full access.

■ BUT WHEN DO STUDENTS MASTER THE MATHEMATICS?

When mathematics is taught in context, mastery takes different forms. Students need time and experience with the ideas of the units. They may not seem to understand all the concepts right away. In the long run, however, mastery will be achieved at a deeper level of understanding. We believe that students will be better able to use and remember what they have learned.

Entry levels

Each unit has a range of entry levels. Some tasks might be more appropriate for students who already have some knowledge of the ideas, but all students can succeed with the work, especially in heterogeneous groups with rich discussions.

Sharing ideas

It's valuable to have students share ideas with their groups and with the rest of the class. This generates discussion and more ideas and inspires others to try new processes. While a report is being presented, other students (and we adults) should concentrate on what is being shared, not on other work.

Critical feedback

Students should be able to constructively discuss strengths and weaknesses of their own and others' work. A safe classroom environment allows students to give each other critical feedback.

▪ WORKING IN GROUPS

Here are some ideas to help the success of cooperative groups:

Develop a feeling of community with the whole group

Allow times for social events or activities to take place where students must interact with other classmates to find out about one another in activities not related to mathematics. Incorporate the origins and multicultural applications of the mathematics you are investigating or exploring.

Create a "team" feeling for temporary groups

Have students stay in the same working group for the duration of each unit. This may be for two to four or five weeks at a time. Have them create team names based on the math ideas of the unit. Have students present their work as a team.

Provide a safe environment for taking risks

Give students specific feedback about their contributions to the group. Take advantage of "anonymous" mistakes to use them as learning opportunities in clarifying ideas. Focus on the error, not on the person. Avoid publicly correcting second-language learners' pronunciation or use of language. In students' writing about mathematics, focus on the ideas instead of the spelling or grammar.

Encourage positive interdependence

In giving specific feedback to individuals, state why the skill or action is important, how it helps the group, and why it is important in adult work. For example: "Xavier, I noticed how quick and accurate you are at visualizing how the angle paths will look when they are drawn. Many architects have the same ability. It is important to their work." Refer other students to Xavier as a resource when they ask for help. Let students be accountable for asking for help from, and giving help to, one another. This process can nurture a high level of trust and respect for each others' contributions and skills. It will also help equalize status issues that may arise.

Establish heterogeneous groups

All students bring skills and experience. Multi-ability, language, and diversity can teach everyone something. Do not make tasks and expectations simpler, but do use varying techniques so that all may have access to the ideas you want the group to explore.

■ LANGUAGE

Children need language to learn and to develop and refine their understanding; discussion during all stages of mathematical learning is important. They need an environment that encourages them to use language to investigate, question, describe, explain, and report.

The units integrate language, writing, and hands-on work in a group setting. They develop higher-order thinking for second-language learners as well as other students. Investigations can be used effectively in bilingual or multilingual classrooms once we accommodate the needs of language minority students.

Context Clues

It's not necessary to simplify the vocabulary or "water down" the content. In fact, it's important to retain complexity. We need, however, to provide verbal, visual, and physical clues to help students make connections.

The unit themes themselves provide frameworks for understanding. We can also paraphrase, compare and contrast, give origin information, encourage informal definitions, and include examples.

As new terms are used, add them to a wall-chart glossary, with short definitions and diagrams. When new topics arise, we can ask students to discuss them in their groups, then with the whole class. When students give presentations with overhead projectors or other visual aids, other students will learn.

Prior Knowledge

Socioeconomic, linguistic, and cultural backgrounds affect prior knowledge. Having students start by writing or telling what they already know helps us know where to begin each unit or lesson and where to make adjustments.

Discussion and Interaction

When people use language to interact, they do many things to facilitate comprehension; they question, repeat, paraphrase, expand on ideas and so on. Discussion and interaction allow learners to explore their thinking with the input and ideas of others. Students negotiate meaning with one another as well as with the teacher.

Debriefing

Debriefing enables students to learn about how they learn (metacognition) as they:

- reflect on their learning experiences,
- extend and deepen understandings, and
- attach personal meaning to the experience.

To facilitate debriefing, students can keep journals, logs, or portfolios. Personal processing occurs immediately; group processing may be done the next day.

■ ASSESSMENT

For this kind of learning it will not be possible to settle for traditional multiple-choice or true-false tests. We need to assess the processes students are using as well as their problem solutions. Current mathematics involves trying multiple paths to multiple solutions.

Communication

Students need to be able to communicate. In the world of work this is a vital skill and is part of working with others. Some important points:

- Communication begins with discussion in groups, with "homework partners," with the whole class, with parents, and with experts outside the classroom.
- Encourage students to use their own language.
- Writing is essential. Students should be able to move from the hasty thoughts of rough drafts to organized and coherent text. Punctuation and spelling are not the "point"—they are a means to clear communication of ideas.
- But don't limit students to writing. Diagrams, drawings, and posters can be the pictures worth 1000 words.
- Oral reports, exhibits, videotapes, and drama encourage students' creativity. Make the math and the math class unforgettable!

Assessment tools

Some of the assessment tools we can use:

- Record observations or interviews, particularly as students work in groups or during oral reports. See pages 22-25 in *Assessment Alternatives in Mathematics* for a list of observation and questioning suggestions.
- Select a regular assignment to collect from all students and use for assessment. Some are identified in the text, but other assignments

could also be used, depending on what you wish to know about students' work.

- Collect portfolios of student work that reveal what they know, can do, or are learning.

Most important, involve all students in the assessment process. One of the greatest advantages we can provide students is the habit of looking at and evaluating their own work. Some ideas:

- Have students help define the standards for good work.
- Help students become familiar with the characteristics of good work (see pages 17-19 in *Assessment Alternatives in Mathematics*). They should become familiar with standards and rubrics, even devising their own rubrics (see appendix *Judging Quality—Rubrics for Investigations Units*).
- Provide anonymous examples of good, mediocre, and poor work. Trade with another teacher, or use papers from past classes. Have students compare, rate, and discuss the papers.
- Encourage a continuous revising process, so that students will:

  look ahead, anticipate, and plan;

  describe their processes and progress as they work;

  reflect on their work, looking for what's well-done and what needs more work;

  not be satisfied with just getting through with the task, but persist, revise, try to pose a next question, ask themselves "What if we did this...?"

As you begin, don't try to do everything at once. Look for one important thing to assess and identify a sensible way to assess it. Just as students need to discuss their work with others, so do you. Find a colleague with whom to talk about what you are doing.

■ GRADES

In each unit, traditional unit tests are replaced by work on an individual project. To evaluate the work and knowledge of students, assessment techniques mentioned above should be utilized throughout the unit.

In assessing their own projects, students should have access to their notes and the work done during the unit. Provide them with situations where they can work in collaborative groups with their peers. Encourage them to cite specific examples from their work to support what they say.

It has not been customary in school for students to be given the opportunity to revise their work; they are usually graded on a first draft. Is it any wonder they believe teachers are content to receive an unfinished product? Just as most of us need feedback and time to revise, we urge that this be a regular part of homework and classwork.

To validate the notion that each student is accountable for his/her own work, it is suggested that the individual projects be given a greater value than other parts of the units. A possible weighting system:

50% Individual project

25% Group Investigation

25% Any other work in unit

■ MANIPULATIVES

Mathematics can be and should be exciting for students. It gives them the tools for solving real problems and a way of looking at their world. If students are to achieve their potential, they must find their mathematics experiences useful, interesting, and relevant to them.

The big picture of mathematics includes thinking in a mathematical way as well as concepts and skills. To impose rules, formulas, and abstract ideas on students before they're ready or before they've had sufficient concrete experiences, discussion, and opportunities to make their own generalizations not only will prove nonproductive, but will stifle the students' development of mathematical understanding.

The *Investigation Units* embed skills and concepts in a context with meaning and purpose. Placing the tasks in a familiar context that makes sense to the students enables them to perform similar tasks in unfamiliar contexts.

Part of promoting equity in the classroom is recognizing that there are as many kinds of thinking and learning styles as there are people. Some people feel comfortable doing the problems in their head; others have to talk about it with their friends. Some students draw pictures, write a list, build it with blocks, plug in a formula, or grab a calculator. These are not crutches meant to be given up once a concept is learned, but are important problem-solving tools.

Students who learn to understand in many ways develop a stronger mathematical sense. A student who may be able to "do it in her head" can develop new comprehension from diagrams and physical materials.

Some students will not have had previous access to manipulatives and will need time to explore. This is time well spent, and it is the intent of the units to approach the mathematical concepts with the use of manipulatives.

Encouraging the use of a broad range of tools will help insure that all learners will have what they need to explore and express their thinking. Words, pencils, numbers, toothpicks, blocks, and calculators help make sense of things that are abstract. These tools should be readily available at all times to all students.

■ CALCULATORS

A tool that is used extensively in society is the calculator. Calculators open up possibilities, promote self discovery, and provide another venue for students whose strength is not necessarily computation. They can help students move more quickly through simple arithmetic tasks and go farther in their thinking about richer mathematics.

Students are best prepared for the future by learning when and how to use a variety of calculators effectively. They must increase their ability to estimate and to judge the reasonableness of the results. These skills accompany the development of understanding of operations and knowing basic facts.

Ideally each student should have his/her own calculator, especially when working on individual projects. During group work provide at least two calculators for each group of four to six students. Encouraging calculator use in the classroom gives students the opportunity to practice and gain experience in using technology.

■ THE FUTURE

The *Investigation Units* were conceived and designed in response to a strong call from business and education for change in mathematics curriculum and instruction. We cannot afford to lose a single student. Changing the way we look at student learning of mathematics can have a profound effect on every child's future as well as the future of our community.

The National Council of Teachers of Mathematics *Curriculum and Evaluation Standards for School Mathematics* (p. 4) says:

> *The social injustices of past schooling practices can no longer be tolerated. Current statistics indicate that those who study advanced mathematics are most often white males. Women and most minorities study less mathematics and are seriously underrepresented in careers using science and technology. Creating a just society in which women and various ethnic groups enjoy equal opportunities and equitable treatment is no longer an issue. Mathematics has become a critical filter for employment and full participation in our society. We cannot afford to have the majority of our population mathematically illiterate: Equity has become an economic necessity.*

TELLING SOMEONE WHERE TO GO

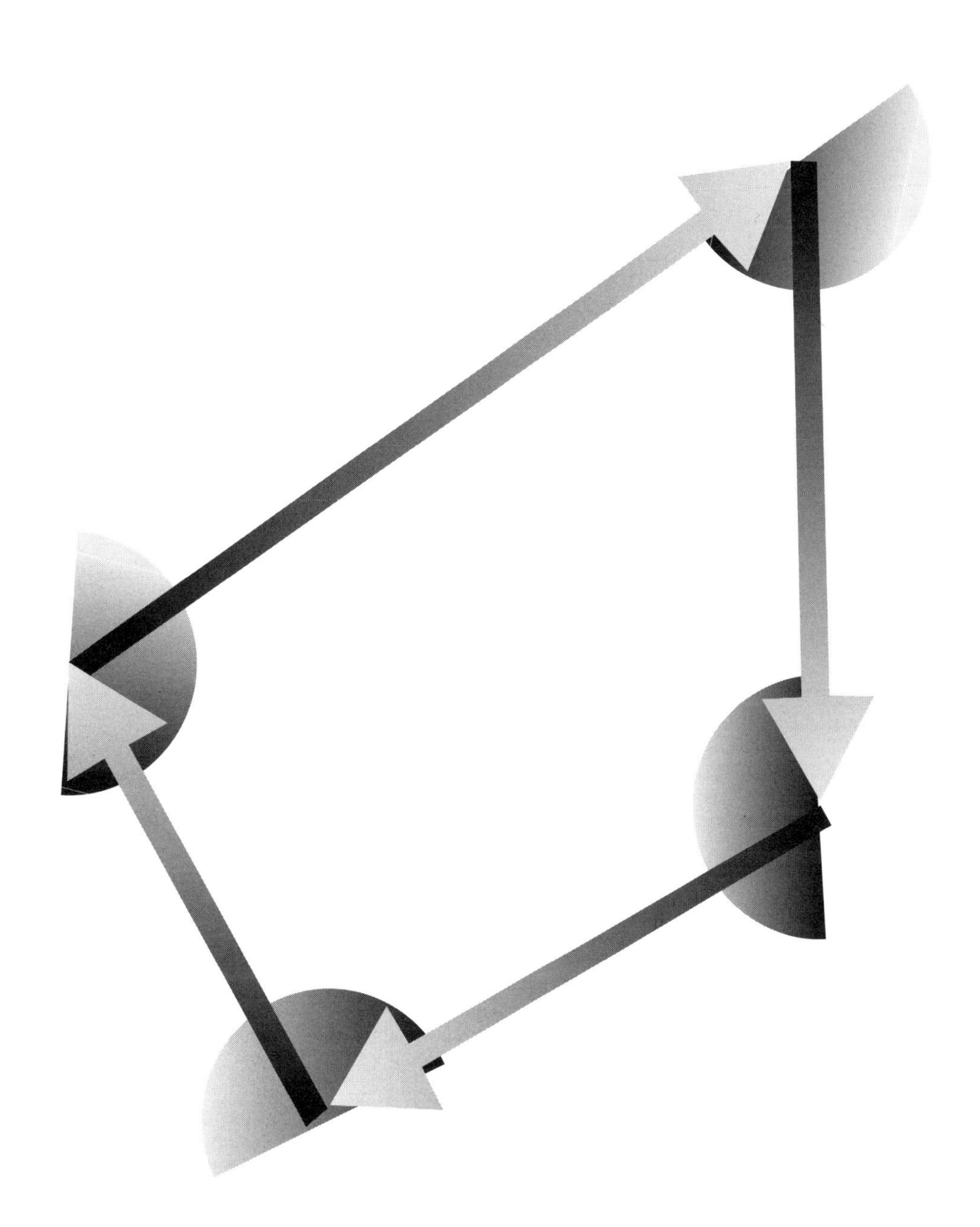

Unit Overview

Measurement of Distance and Angle

In this unit the mathematics of navigation is studied in the spirit of the wilderness sport of orienteering. To navigate from one place to another, headings and distances will be measured. However, magnetic compasses are not used in this unit. Instead, headings are specified in degrees of a turn left or right, as measured from straight ahead. To solve some of the orienteering problems, students must accurately pace out distances and turn their bodies to specified angle headings.

A secondary emphasis of the unit explores the effects on paths when each of the legs are multiplied by the same number or when the same length is added to each leg.

In this unit students will be challenged to:

- give clear written and oral directional instructions;
- create and follow orienteering paths using angle-ometers, paces, meter-cords and;
- draw scale maps of paths using protractors and rulers;
- investigate what happens to paths when distances are scaled up or down by multiplying, and by adding.

The Individual Investigation of session 7 involves students analyzing the effects of using faulty measuring tools when drawing closed paths.

The unit can be completed over a period of four to five weeks, or may be spread out over a longer time span with other work interspersed between sessions. The first two sessions are best done where there is lots of space, preferably outdoors, so it is best to plan on using the unit in the fall or spring.

■ MATHEMATICAL OBJECTIVES

Students will:

- make meter cords and use them to measure and lay out distances accurately to the nearest tenth of a meter.
- use a centimeter ruler to measure and draw lengths to the nearest tenth of a centimeter.
- use an angle-ometer to estimate turns to the nearest ten degrees.
- use a protractor to measure and draw angles to the nearest degree.

Students will also undertake investigations to explore the following relationships:

- how adding a constant length to each leg of a shape in most cases distorts the shape.
- how multiplying all the legs of a shape by a constant factor preserves the original shape.

■ MATHEMATICAL ISSUES

Telling someone how to get somewhere usually involves specifying two quantities: distance and heading.

Distance can be measured in standard units such as inches, meters, or miles, or in non-standard units such as paces or city blocks. Heading is defined by the amount of turn, or angle. The angle can be specified as a turn from a standard direction, such as "north," or as a turn from the relative direction which you are currently facing.

Examples of standard directional systems include: magnetic compass headings such as "Northeast," which means turn 45 degrees clockwise from due North, and Cartesian coordinate systems where the positive x-axis points to 0° and angles are measured counterclockwise from this axis. In later mathematics courses, vector headings are usually described using a standard directional system.

In *Telling Someone Where To Go* we will not be using a standard directional system. Instead, headings will be given using a relative directional system. Each new heading is determined by an amount of turn from the direction you are facing prior to the turn. In the computer language LOGO, instructions are written to describe paths that a "turtle" will follow. Headings for the turtle are given relative to the direction the turtle is currently pointing. Other examples of this type of heading include: directions for getting around in a city such as "turn right" or "turn left" from the direction you are going, and "clock directions" such as "5 o'clock," with 12 o'clock being straight ahead.

The LOGO-style method for specifying directions was chosen for this unit for two reasons. First, non-standard units are widely used in everyday life and are more easily understood by middle school students. The more rigid standard units inrtroduce a technical level that might interfere with the basic mathematical understandings of this unit. Second, we want the unit to be undertaken without having to purchase a class set of expensive magnetic compasses. Third, the work of this unit may be tied to prior LOGO experiences. Although the use of computers and LOGO is not necessary, they can be used as tools in student investigations.

When describing or following a path in this unit, each heading given will be measured from the direction you are facing just before you turn.

Assessment

Assessment should be an integral part of teaching. It is the mechanism whereby teachers can learn how students think about mathematics as well as what students are able to accomplish.

—Everybody Counts, *MSEB, 1990; p. 69*

In this *Investigations Unit* we want to assess students' abilities to:

- describe mathematical ideas orally and in writing,
- draw and interpret diagrams,
- explain and defend logical arguments,
- design and carry out experiments to test a hypothesis,
- collect, organize, and generalize from data,
- develop mathematical approaches to make sense of a new situation, and
- identify and summarize major ideas.

Each *Investigations Unit* culminates in an Individual Project. It provides an important indicator of each student's mathematical growth, skill, and understanding. The Individual Project particularly fits the kind of assessment described in *Assessment Alternatives in Mathematics* (Jean Stenmark, EQUALS Lawrence Hall Of Science, 1989):

In mathematics we need assessment that:

- *matches the ideal curriculum as described in the California Mathematics Framework and the NCTM Standards in both what is taught and how it is experienced, with thoughtful questions that allow for thoughtful responses.*
- *communicates to students, teachers, and parents that most real problems cannot be solved quickly and that many have more than one answer.*
- *allows students to learn at their own pace.*
- *focuses on what students do know and can do rather than what they don't know.*
- *won't label half of students as failures because their scores aren't above the 50th percentile OR*
- *doesn't rely on the traditional bell shape curve to rank students.*
- *doesn't use time as a factor, since speed is almost never relevant in mathematical effectiveness.*
- *is integral to instruction and doesn't detract from students' opportunities to continue to learn.*

Having each student keep a portfolio will facilitate assessment of work produced during the unit. Tasks within the unit provide a wide range of contexts for examining student thinking including written reports, models, diagrams, group work, experiments, and projects.

Unless a student's work on the Individual Project is counted heavily in determining the letter grade, the project will not have the perceived value of other activities. Therefore, the following weights for determining a letter grade are suggested:

40%	Individual Project
30%	Group Projects (all group members receive the same grade)
30%	All other work in the unit

Structuring Group Work

Many activities in this unit are intended for students working in groups. Some research indicates that groups of four or five are ideal. Initially these groups can be assigned by shuffling cards, or some other random method. As groups change you may want to create a structure that guarantees that students have the opportunity to work with as many classmates as possible throughout the year.

■ SUCCESSFUL STUDENT INTERACTION

Emphasize to students that everyone in the group is responsible for working together to contribute ideas and get results. One way to do this is to get students to generate a list of what they think are the characteristics of a successful team. After they have given general ideas, ask them to think of what they need personally to feel included and safe in a working group. A poster of the ideas can be displayed as reminders and standards for the class. Discussion of the implications of these three rules (adapted from Stanford University's Center for Complex Instruction) gives students a structure for group interactions:

Student Group Work Guidelines

1. You have the duty to assist anyone in your group who asks for help.

2. You have the right to ask anyone in your group for help.

3. When helping others, help them without doing things for them.

Roles

Assigning a different role to each group member promotes cooperation and inclusion and allows students to assume the various responsibilities necessary for completing the task.

Suggested roles are: spokesperson, recorder, moderator, and technician.

Spokesperson–organizes and presents the group's project orally to the rest of the class and answers questions.

Moderator–responsible for keeping the group on task. This person makes sure that everyone has had an opportunity to contribute ideas. If they have exhausted group resources, during work, the moderator may ask the teacher questions on behalf of the group.

Recorder–writes down and organizes information the group decides on, writes up charts/transparencies for use during oral presentation.

Technician–responsible for getting equipment and supplies as needed, organizing clean-up (everyone cleans), making sure calculators are put away. Materials should be kept on an accessible shelf or supply area that all students can reach easily.

Reviewer–(optional) checks worksheets (if applicable) and makes sure that all group members have done their work and initials the completed worksheets. The reviewer does NOT make corrections or judgments about the work. This process encourages all students to do the work, and share information with those who may not have understood the problems posed.

Rotating Roles

Each student should assume one role at a time. Occasionally one student may take two roles if someone is absent. Although groups may stay together for the entire unit, roles within the group should be rotated among all group members as they work on different projects. Some teachers rotate the jobs daily, others do so weekly. What is important is that all students have the opportunity to perform all the roles. It is important that each student have an opportunity to develop the skills and abilities needed to carry out each role.

* *See "Working in Groups" in the Introduction, p. x.*

Description of Sessions, Time, and Materials Needed

SESSION AND TIME	DESCRIPTION	MATERIALS NEEDED
1 1 hour Page 15	*Walking Paths With the Angle-ometer, Day 1 and Day 2* Students walk and sketch paths using paces to measure distance and angle-ometers to measure headings. Angle is experienced as an amount of turn from straight ahead, measured in degrees to the left or right.	For each student: *Letter to Family* (p. 55) *Angle-ometer* (p. 57) *Walking Paths Homework* (p. 63) For each pair of students: *Walking Paths With the Angle-ometer #1* (p. 59) *Walking Paths With the Angle-ometer #2* (p. 61)
2 2 hours Page 20	*Precision Orienteering With Meter-cord* Students make a meter-cord and use it, along with the angle-ometer, to lay out paths accurately. Given three legs of a closed path, students lay out the path and measure the distance and heading for the fourth leg in order to return to the starting point.	For each pair of students: 5 meters of cord, a meter stick, masking tape and/or a felt-tip marking pen, *Getting Around: Orienteering Worksheet* (p. 69), and *Getting Around: Orienteering Paths,* cut apart and stored in envelopes (pp. 65, 67)
3 1 hour Page 25	*Orienteering On Paper With Protractors* Students relate the angle-ometer to the protractor. Students use the protractor and centimeter ruler to lay out closed paths to scale on paper. Students create problems for other students to solve.	For each student: A protractor, centimeter ruler, and several sheets of unlined paper For the teacher: A transparent protractor and centimeter ruler for overhead projector demonstration.

SESSION AND TIME	DESCRIPTION	MATERIALS NEEDED
 1 hour Page 28	*Angle Check* "Angle check" for closed paths is introduced to enable students to determine the accuracy of their angle measurements for themselves.	For each student: Calculator
 2 hours Page 33	*Navigating in the Dark (Optional)* Students gain more practice using a protractor and ruler. Students, working in groups, write instructions for a path to safely navigate in the dark without running into obstacles. Following instructions, another group of students draw the path, without knowing the location of the obstacles. Afterwards, a third group of students take on the role of "investigative reporters." The "reporters" write an analysis of the accuracy of the original instructions, and how well they were followed by the second group.	Introduction Option 1 For each pair of students: centimeter ruler, protractor *Demo Map* (p. 73) *Navigating Homework* (pp. 91, 93) Introduction Option 2 For each student or pair of students: centimeter ruler, protractor blank transparency, overhead pen *Navigation Sheets* (2) (pp. 75–80) For each student: *Navigation Sheets* (3) (pp. 75–80) For each group of students: 4 copies of *Navigation Sheets* (pp. 75–80) *Navigational Masters Series* (p. 97) *Navigating in the Dark,* maps 1-5 (pp. 81–90) 4 or 5 business-sized envelopes glue, scissors For the teacher transparencies of: *Demo Map* (p. 73) *Navigation Sheets* (2) (pp. 75–80) *Exxon Valdez Articles* (p. 71) *Demo Map* (p. 73) *Navigating in the Dark,* maps 1-5 (pp. 81–90) *Navigation in the Dark* *Instructions for the Investigation Reporter* (p. 95) *Navigational Masters Series* (p. 97) *Homework* (pp. 91–93) transparent protractor, transparent centimeter ruler, overhead pen

SESSION AND TIME	DESCRIPTION	MATERIALS NEEDED
6	*Changes in Paths Resulting From Changes in Lengths* *Ratio Check*	For each student: A protractor, centimeter ruler, and calculator
2 hours	The skills learned in sessions 1 through 4 are used to investigate what happens when all the legs of a path are enlarged by adding the same length to each leg or by multiplying each leg length by the same number.	For the teacher transparency: *Changes in Paths Resulting From Changes in Lengths* (p. 99)
Page 40	A "Ratio Check" to test for similar paths is introduced.	
7	*Group Investigation Project: What Happens To Paths When Leg Lengths Are Changed?*	For each student: Mathematics Toolkit
3 hours	This is an extension of the investigation begun in session 5. Groups research what happens when their assigned path is enlarged by adding and by multiplying. Groups present their findings to the rest of the class.	For each group of students: *Group Investigation Assignment* (p. 105) *Paths For Group Investigations* (p. 103) *Step-by-Step Guide For Doing the Group Investigation* (p. 107)—optional poster paper or transparencies, pens, rulers, protractors, calculators For the teacher transparencies of: *Group Investigation Assignment* (p. 105) *Paths For Group Investigations* (p. 103)
Page 44	Students summarize their discoveries by writing ideas in their own Mathematics Toolkit.	

SESSION AND TIME	DESCRIPTION	MATERIALS NEEDED
 5 hours total Page 49	*Individual Investigation Project: Analyzing the Effects of Faulty Measuring Tools* Students take on the role of employees of an orienteering company. The president of the company asks the employees to 1) investigate the effects of using faulty tools mistakenly manufactured and distributed 2) write a report to be sent to the customers.	For each student: *Individual Project: Analyzing the Effects of Faulty Measuring Tools* (p. 109) *Individual Project Self-Evaluation* (p. 111)
9 2 hours Page 57	*Sharing Individual Projects* *End-of-unit Assessment* *Seminar Questions* provides a format for students to share their individual projects. An optional end-of-unit written assessment is included.	For each student: *End-of-unit Assessment* (p. 117) For each group of students: *Individual Investigation Seminar Questions* (p. 115)

* *Total time required for the unit: approximately 19 hours (four to five weeks).*

INVESTIGATIONS

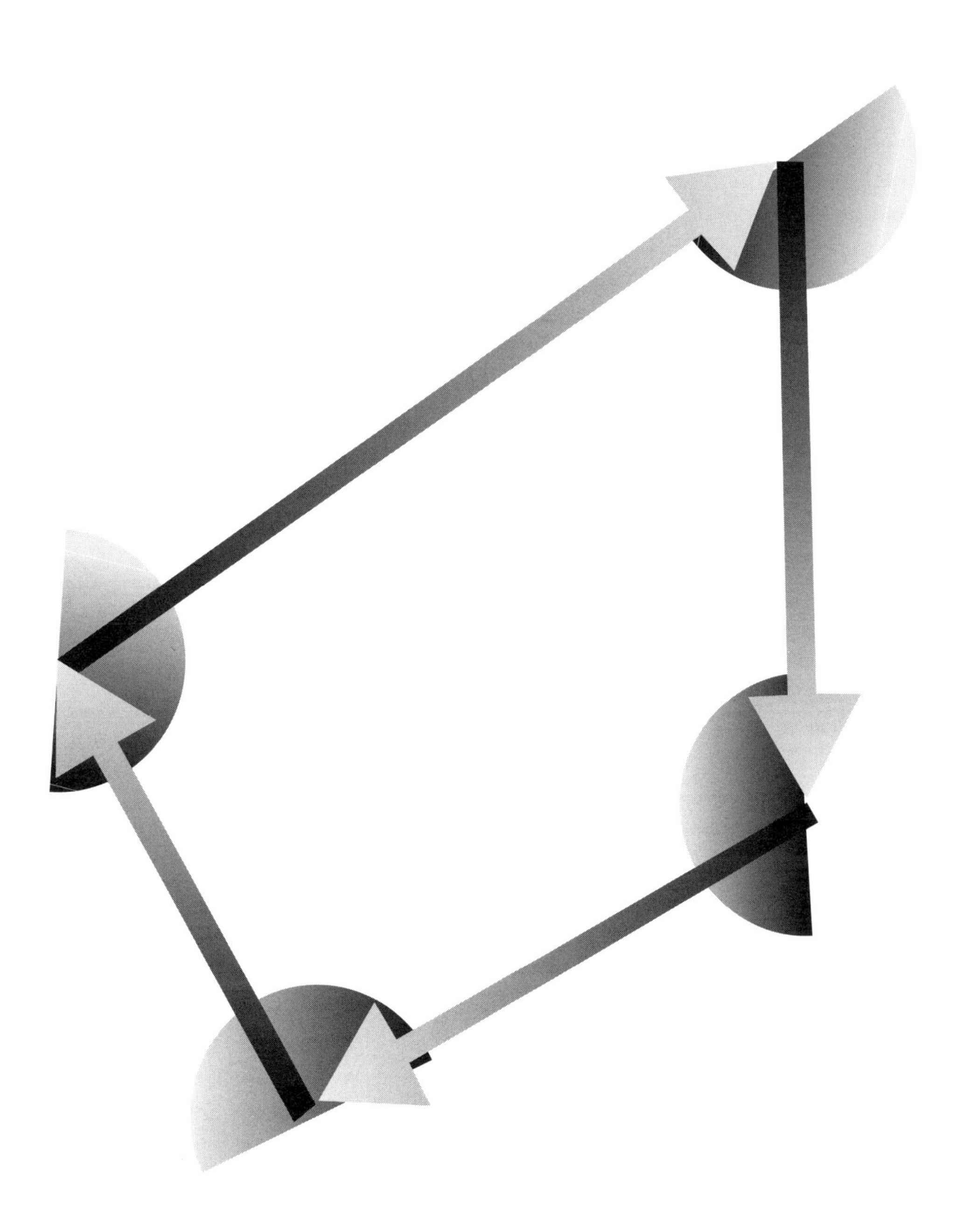

1 Walking Paths With the Angle-ometer
Letter to Family

■ **LETTER TO FAMILY**

The letter provided is meant to be given to students and their parents at the beginning of the unit. When parents are kept informed, they usually are very supportive.

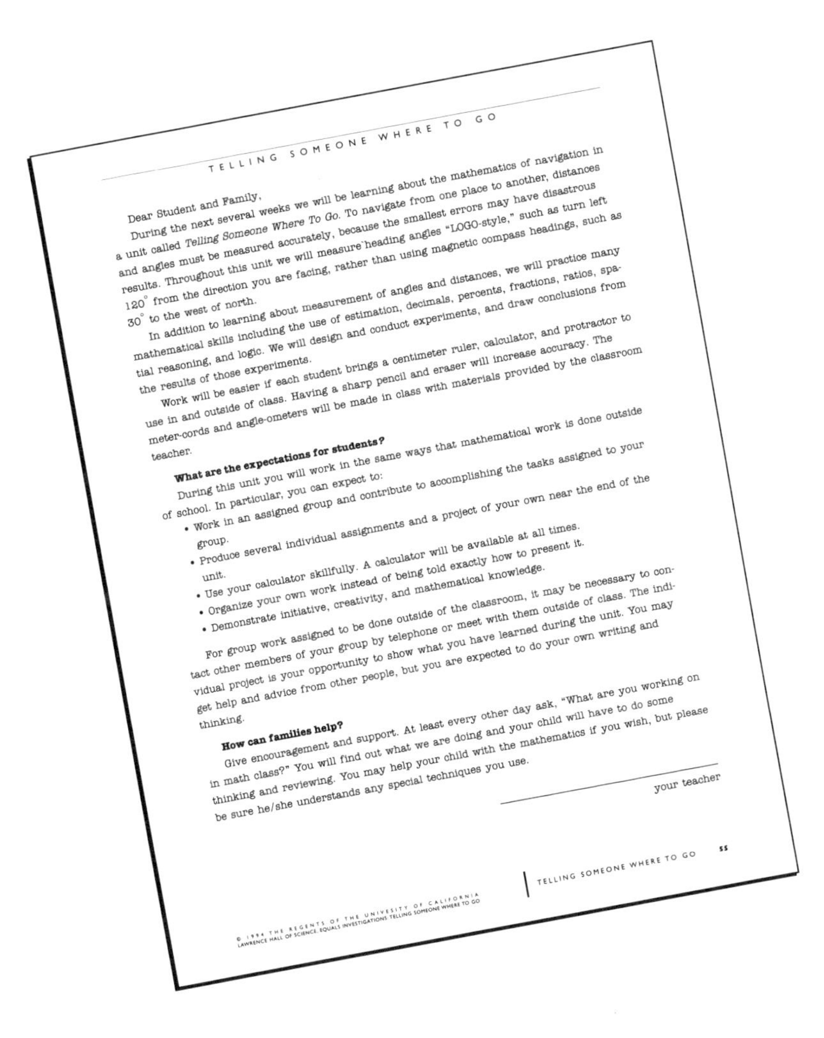

TELLING SOMEONE WHERE TO GO

Dear Student and Family,

During the next several weeks we will be learning about the mathematics of navigation in a unit called *Telling Someone Where To Go*. To navigate from one place to another, distances and angles must be measured accurately, because the smallest errors may have disastrous results. Throughout this unit we will measure heading angles "LOGO-style," such as turn left 120° from the direction you are facing, rather than using magnetic compass headings, such as 30° to the west of north.

In addition to learning about measurement of angles and distances, we will practice many mathematical skills including the use of estimation, decimals, percents, fractions, ratios, spatial reasoning, and logic. We will design and conduct experiments, and draw conclusions from the results of those experiments.

Work will be easier if each student brings a centimeter ruler, calculator, and protractor to use in and outside of class. Having a sharp pencil and eraser will increase accuracy. The meter-cords and angle-ometers will be made in class with materials provided by the classroom teacher.

What are the expectations for students?

During this unit you will work in the same ways that mathematical work is done outside of school. In particular, you can expect to:

- Work in an assigned group and contribute to accomplishing the tasks assigned to your group.
- Produce several individual assignments and a project of your own near the end of the unit.
- Use your calculator skillfully. A calculator will be available at all times.
- Organize your own work instead of being told exactly how to present it.
- Demonstrate initiative, creativity, and mathematical knowledge.

For group work assigned to be done outside of the classroom, it may be necessary to contact other members of your group by telephone or meet with them outside of class. The individual project is your opportunity to show what you have learned during the unit. You may get help and advice from other people, but you are expected to do your own writing and thinking.

How can families help?

Give encouragement and support. At least every other day ask, "What are you working on in math class?" You will find out what we are doing and your child will have to do some thinking and reviewing. You may help your child with the mathematics if you wish, but please be sure he/she understands any special techniques you use.

____
your teacher

TELLING SOMEONE WHERE TO GO 55

Getting Ready

The tasks in this first session lay the intuitive groundwork for future work requiring greater precision and abstraction. In this session students will pace off distances and turn their bodies to line up with headings. Distance and angle measure are experienced in an egocentric, kinesthetic way.

- **MATERIALS:** Walking Paths With the Angle-ometer #1 *(p. 59)*, Walking Paths With the Angle-ometer #2 *(p. 61)*, Letter to Family *(p. 55)*, Angle-ometer *(p. 57)*, Walking Paths With the Angle-ometer Homework *(p. 63)*.
- **TIME:** *1 hour*

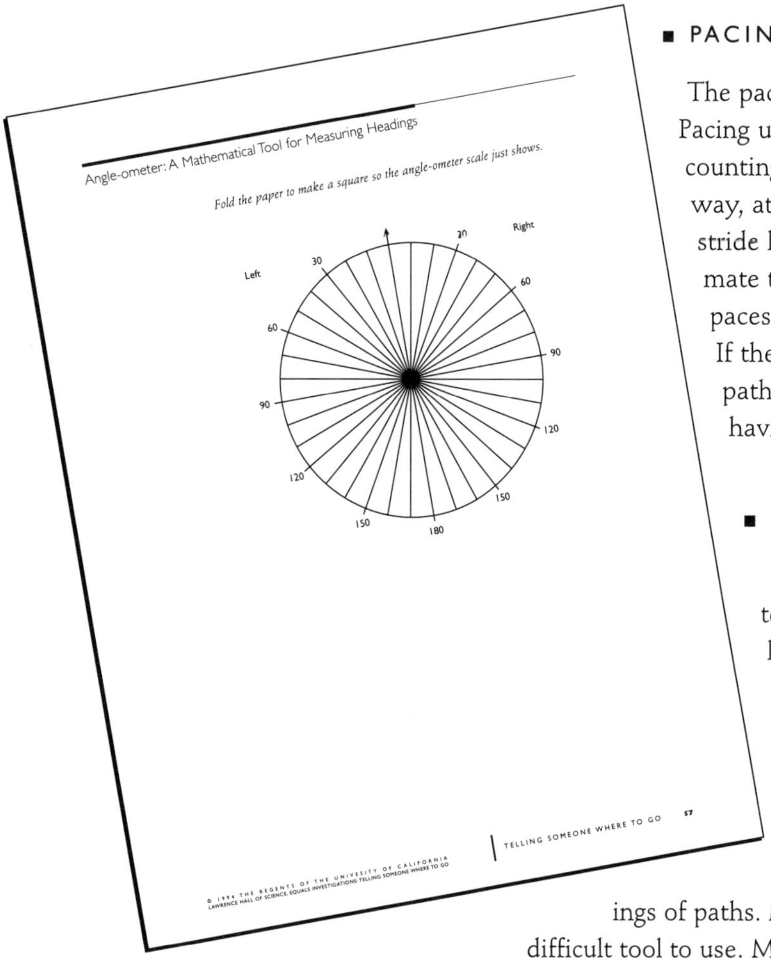

■ PACING OFF DISTANCE

The pace is a convenient unit for measuring distances. Pacing usually means walking in a natural fashion and counting the strides taken. If students walk in a relaxed way, at a constant speed, and on a uniform surface, their stride lengths will stay consistent. Ask students to estimate the width of the classroom measured in their own paces and have them pace it off to check their estimates. If the weather is bad and the class can't go outside, the paths can be made smaller and paced off inside by having students use toe-to-heel-style strides.

■ HEADINGS WITH THE ANGLE-OMETER

When giving people directions, it is not enough to tell them how far they must go; they also need to know the direction in which to head. Give each student a copy of the angle-ometer. The angle-ometer paper should be folded to make it smaller and stiffer. In session 2 the angle-ometer will be used to lay out orienteering paths.

In session 3, protractors will be substituted for the angle-ometers to make more accurate drawings of paths. Many middle school students find the protractor a difficult tool to use. Measuring angles with the angle-ometer helps students make sense of the protractor.

Heading Practice

Ask all students to stand up, hold their angle-ometer in front of them, and face the same starting direction. Before each turn, 0° will be straight ahead. This is the LOGO-style way of giving directions.

Ask everyone to turn Left 60°. Wait until students turn before you turn, otherwise they'll copy you without thinking. Ask everyone where

0° is now. Answer: STRAIGHT AHEAD! Ask them to turn Right 180°. Then Left 120°. They should all be facing the original direction.

Try a few more turns with them until most students can use the angle-ometer to find headings. The most common difficulty at this point is forgetting that 0° is always the direction you are facing just before making each new turn.

Walking Paths With the Angle-ometer #1

Pair students up and give each team one of the *Walking Paths With the Angle-ometer #1* sheets. It is important that students walk the paths together so they can discuss what they are doing. Giving one instruction sheet per team will encourage discussion and cooperation.

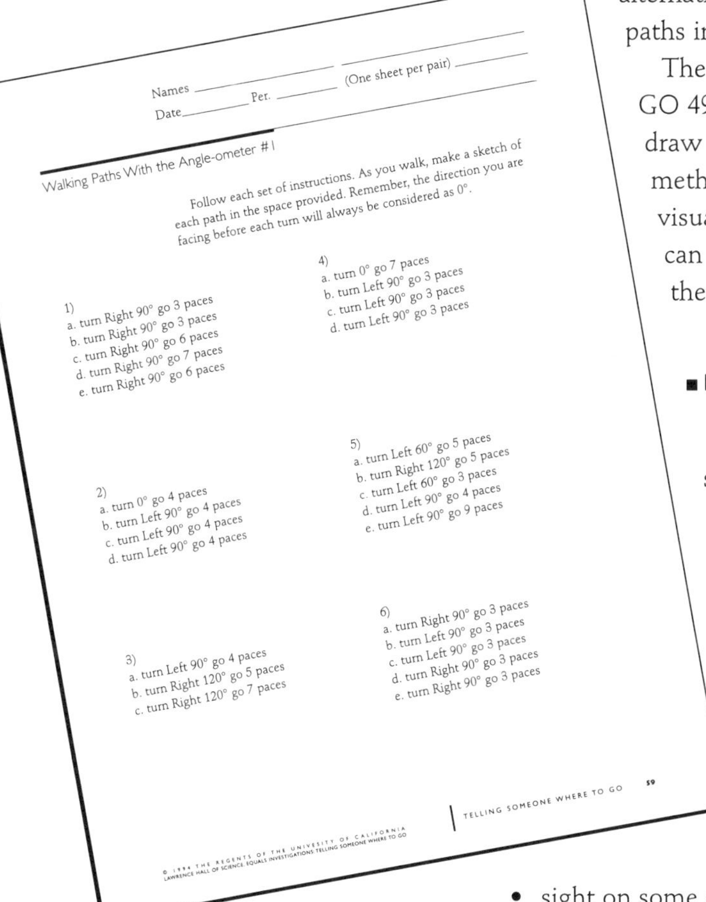

Names ______ (One sheet per pair) ______
Date______ Per. ______

Walking Paths With the Angle-ometer #1

Follow each set of instructions. As you walk, make a sketch of each path in the space provided. Remember, the direction you are facing before each turn will always be considered as 0°.

1)
a. turn Right 90° go 3 paces
b. turn Right 90° go 3 paces
c. turn Right 90° go 6 paces
d. turn Right 90° go 7 paces
e. turn Right 90° go 6 paces

2)
a. turn 0° go 4 paces
b. turn Left 90° go 4 paces
c. turn Left 90° go 4 paces
d. turn Left 90° go 4 paces

3)
a. turn Left 90° go 4 paces
b. turn Right 120° go 5 paces
c. turn Right 120° go 7 paces

4)
a. turn 0° go 7 paces
b. turn Left 90° go 3 paces
c. turn Left 90° go 3 paces
d. turn Left 90° go 3 paces

5)
a. turn Left 60° go 5 paces
b. turn Right 120° go 5 paces
c. turn Left 60° go 3 paces
d. turn Left 90° go 4 paces
e. turn Left 90° go 9 paces

6)
a. turn Right 90° go 3 paces
b. turn Left 90° go 3 paces
c. turn Left 90° go 3 paces
d. turn Right 90° go 3 paces
e. turn Right 90° go 3 paces

TELLING SOMEONE WHERE TO GO 59

Send pairs of students outside to walk the courses, or alternatively, they can use heel-toe pacing and walk the paths inside. This exercise will take about 20 minutes.

The shapes of the paths give a message. (The message is GO 49RS, but don't tell!) Some students find it difficult to draw a path after they walk it. Let them figure out a method of doing this by themselves—it is a good spatial visualization task. Some students will decide that they can sketch the paths free-hand without actually walking them.

■ PROCESSING WALKING PATHS #1

After walking and sketching the courses, have students share their experiences and discuss the way the team worked together.

Angle-ometer Use. Some students get disorientated when first using the angle-ometer because it turns with them as they turn. Ask if anyone invented or has an idea for efficient ways to use the angle-ometer. Have them share their methods with the class.

Your students will come up with many ideas. Here are some that teachers have shared with us:

- sight on some object at the proper heading before turning;
- set the angle-ometer down on the ground before turning so it won't move;
- put markers on the ground to show where straight ahead is and where the turn ends;
- keep one toe toward 0° and turn the other toe towards the given heading.

Sketching Paths.

Ask if anyone discovered a way to sketch paths so that they accurately resemble the walked paths. Often students sketch the paths so that each pace is recorded as a dash. This is a good first step in understanding the concepts of scaling, similarity, and proportionality. Introduce the terms and concepts in an intuitive way, using explanations such as "shrunk or enlarged" for scaled and "the same shape, but a different size" for similar and proportional.

■ HOMEWORK FOR WALKING PATHS #1

Students should now be ready to write directional instructions for simple paths of their own. Have them write instructions to make a message of their own or to write initials, but limit it to 3 to 6 letters. Ask them to either fold the paper in half and write instructions on the top and solutions on the bottom, or use the front and back. Students can trade papers and try each other's paths tomorrow.

■ PROCESSING HOMEWORK FOR WALKING PATHS #1

Ask two or three students to write their instructions on the board or overhead and have everyone try to figure out what their paths look like without actually pacing them out. Have students pair up and try each other's homework paths.

Names ________ ________ (One sheet per pair) ________
Date________ Per. ________

Walking Paths With the Angle-ometer #2

Follow each set of instructions. As you walk, make a sketch of each path in the space beside the instructions. Remember, the direction you are facing before each turn will always be considered as 0°.

1)
a. turn Right 60° go 10 paces
b. turn Right 120° go 5 paces
c. turn Right 120° go 10 paces
d. turn Left 120° go 5 paces

2)
a. turn Left 60° go 10 paces
b. turn Left 120° go 5 paces
c. turn Left 120° go 10 paces
d. turn Right 120° go 5 paces

3)
a. turn Right 45° go 10 paces
b. turn Right 45° go 7 paces
c. turn Right 90° go 7 paces
d. turn Right 45° go 10 paces
e. turn Right 90° go 10 paces

4)
a. turn 0° go 10 paces
b. turn Left 144° go 10 paces
c. turn Left 144° go 10 paces
d. turn Left 144° go 10 paces
e. turn Left 144° go 10 paces

5)
a. turn Right 45° go 12 paces
b. turn Left 90° go 6 paces
c. turn Left 90° go 6 paces
d. turn Left 90° go 12 paces
e. turn Right 135° go 7 paces

6)
a. turn 0° go 3 paces
b. turn Right 90° go 6 paces
c. turn Left 135° go 8 paces
d. turn Right 135° go 2 paces
e. turn Left 135° go 3 paces
f. turn Left 90° go 3 paces
g. turn Left 135° go 2 paces
h. turn Right 135° go 8 paces
i. turn Left 135° go 6 paces
j. turn Right 90° go 3 paces

Walking Paths With the Angle-ometer #2

This task is for pairs of students. Before beginning, review the discussion from the previous day on how to use the angle-ometer accurately.

■ PROCESSING THE ACTIVITY

At the end of the activity, allow students to share their solutions with each other. The last three are more difficult. Encourage them to talk about strategies and methods used that were improvements over the previous day's work.

This sheet is to be done by individual students.

Problem 1 should give a rough outline of a bird. An interesting extension for some students might be writing another set of instructions for a different animal or shape.

Problem 2 has no starting point designated and no sizing scale given for a pace. Students can choose their starting points and create their own scales.

Problem 3 assesses what students know about rectangles, and whether they can apply their knowledge in the context of orienteering.

Problem 4 write-ups can be used to create more walking paths for other students to follow. The idea of a *Closed Path* will be used throughout the remainder of the unit.

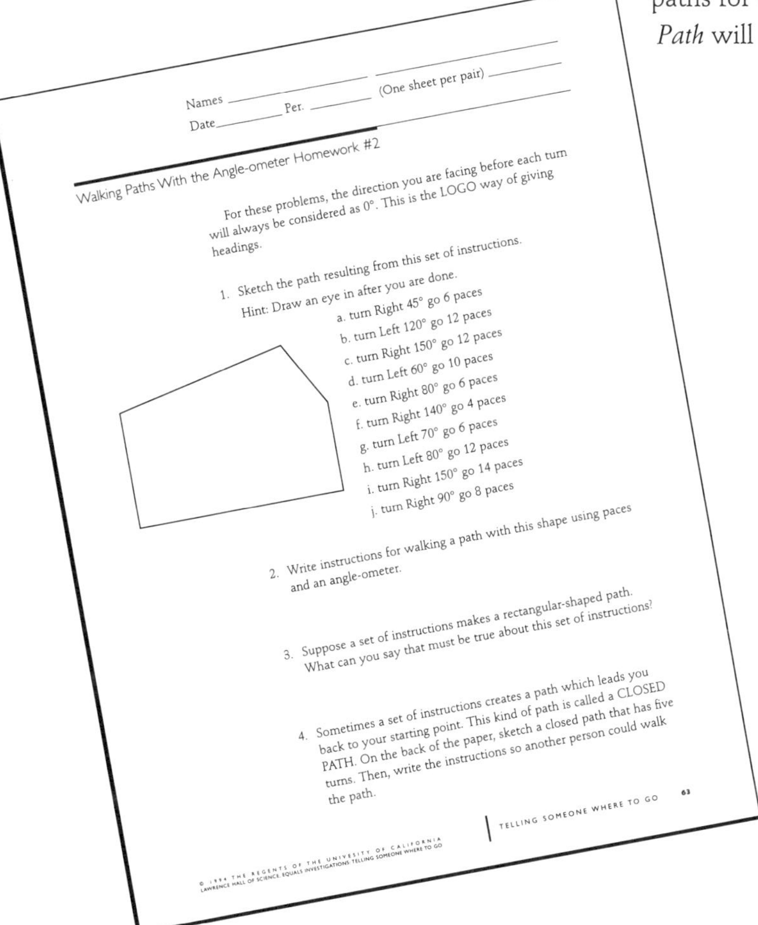

Names ______________ ______________ (One sheet per pair) ______________

Date__________ Per. __________

Walking Paths With the Angle-ometer Homework #2

For these problems, the direction you are facing before each turn will always be considered as 0°. This is the LOGO way of giving headings.

1. Sketch the path resulting from this set of instructions.
   Hint: Draw an eye in after you are done.
   a. turn Right 45° go 6 paces
   b. turn Left 120° go 12 paces
   c. turn Right 150° go 12 paces
   d. turn Left 60° go 10 paces
   e. turn Right 80° go 6 paces
   f. turn Right 140° go 4 paces
   g. turn Left 70° go 6 paces
   h. turn Left 80° go 12 paces
   i. turn Right 150° go 14 paces
   j. turn Right 90° go 8 paces

2. Write instructions for walking a path with this shape using paces and an angle-ometer.

3. Suppose a set of instructions makes a rectangular-shaped path. What can you say that must be true about this set of instructions?

4. Sometimes a set of instructions creates a path which leads you back to your starting point. This kind of path is called a CLOSED PATH. On the back of the paper, sketch a closed path that has five turns. Then, write the instructions so another person could walk the path.

TELLING SOMEONE WHERE TO GO 63

© 1994 THE REGENTS OF THE UNIVERSITY OF CALIFORNIA
LAWRENCE HALL OF SCIENCE, EQUALS INVESTIGATIONS: TELLING SOMEONE WHERE TO GO

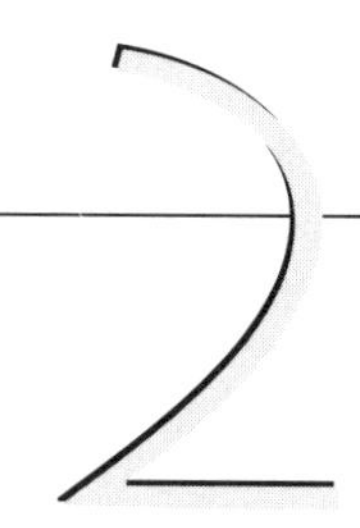

Precision Orienteering With Meter-cord

Orienteering is the sport of following a course over open terrain using only a map and a magnetic compass. Winners are determined by a combination of time and reaching certain designated check-points. In certain respects, orienteering is like a road rally in the woods. The orienteering in *Telling Someone Where To Go* is on a smaller scale.

- MATERIALS: *5 meters of cord (preferably heavy brown hemp or clothesline), a meter stick, masking tape and/or a felt-tip marking pen; student worksheets* Getting Around: Orienteering Worksheet *(p. 69),* Getting Around: Orienteering Paths, *cut apart and stored in envelopes. (pp. 65, 67).*
- TIME: *2 hours*

Getting Around: Orienteering Paths

Students should do *Getting Around: Orienteering Paths (pp. 65, 67)* in teams because use of the meter-cord and an angle-ometer requires the cooperation of two students.

In this task, students are given the first three legs of a closed quadrilateral path. They must lay out the first three legs of the path accurately and then measure the distance and heading for the fourth leg to return to the starting point. A score is determined by comparing student measurements for the fourth leg with the actual distance and heading.

Two versions of this activity are included: one for outside and one for inside. Both versions use the angle-ometer for measuring headings accurate to the nearest ten degrees. The outside version uses the meter-cord to measure distances up to 5 meters to the nearest tenth of a meter and can be done on blacktop (mark with chalk or pennies) or lawn (mark with popsicle stick stakes).

In case of inclement weather, use the inside version on chart paper with meter sticks to measure distances to the nearest tenth meter. Paths for inside are designed to fit onto a piece of chart paper measuring about 60 cm by 90 cm. Courses should be sketched first to make sure the path won't go off the paper.

Making Meter-cords

Students will make meter-cords to measure distances to the nearest tenth of a meter. All distances will be less than 5 meters. Headings will be identified with the angle-ometer.

The best cord material is heavy brown hemp, clothesline cord, or any cord that does not tangle easily. Give each pair a length of cord slightly longer than 5 meters.

To make this easy, find something in the classroom that is longer than five meters, such as the chalkboard tray or tile markings on the floor. Locate yourself at one end of the distance and hold the ball of twine in one hand. Then have one student from each team pull the cord from the ball of twine and walk to the other end of the distance. When the student gets past the five-meter mark, cut the twine. Don't try to cut off exactly 5 meters because the cord is easier to use if it is slightly longer than 5 meters.

Provide meter sticks. Either a felt-tip pen or small pieces of tape may be used to mark the cord in meters. Teachers in foggy locations, warn students that tape slips on damp cord. On the other hand, when students make mistakes, it's easier to correct when tape is used.

Mark the last meter on the cord into tenths of a meter. The cord must be marked carefully so that distances can be measured accurately. After marking it, coil up the cord so it won't become tangled. To identify a team's cord, fasten masking tape on one end with team members' names.

■ CLASS DEMONSTRATION WITH THE SAMPLE PATH

Before students begin orienteering on their own it is a good idea to demonstrate. Either take the class outside, or have students move their desks to the sides of the room. Pick a pair of students and talk them through the sample path below while the others watch. Review notation as you proceed through the demonstration.

SAMPLE PATH (OUTSIDE OPTION)	SAMPLE PATH (INSIDE OPTION)
Mark a starting point with chalk	Mark a starting point with pencil
Go 3 m in any direction	Go 30 cm in any direction
Turn right 90° and go 4 m.	Turn 90° and go 40 cm
Turn right 120° and go 3.5 m.	Turn 120° and go 35 cm

Measure the heading and distance to return to your starting point.

Scoring out of 100 points.

Start with 100 points and deduct

10 points for every whole ten degrees the return heading is off,

1 point for each tenth of a meter that the return distance is off.

If the students' measured return distance is less than a tenth of a meter off and the measured heading is less than 10° off, then a score of 100 is earned.

Evaluate the score so students can see the value of being accurate. For the sample path, the actual measurements of the last leg to return to the starting point should be

Right 60°, go 2.25 m.
(for the inside version, Right 60°, go 22.5 cm.)

Suppose the sample path above is laid out and the measurements taken for the fourth leg are:

turn Right 47° and go 2.6 m

The score would be 87, since 10 points would be deducted for the heading being off by 13° and 3 points would be deducted for being 3 tenths of a meter off in distance.

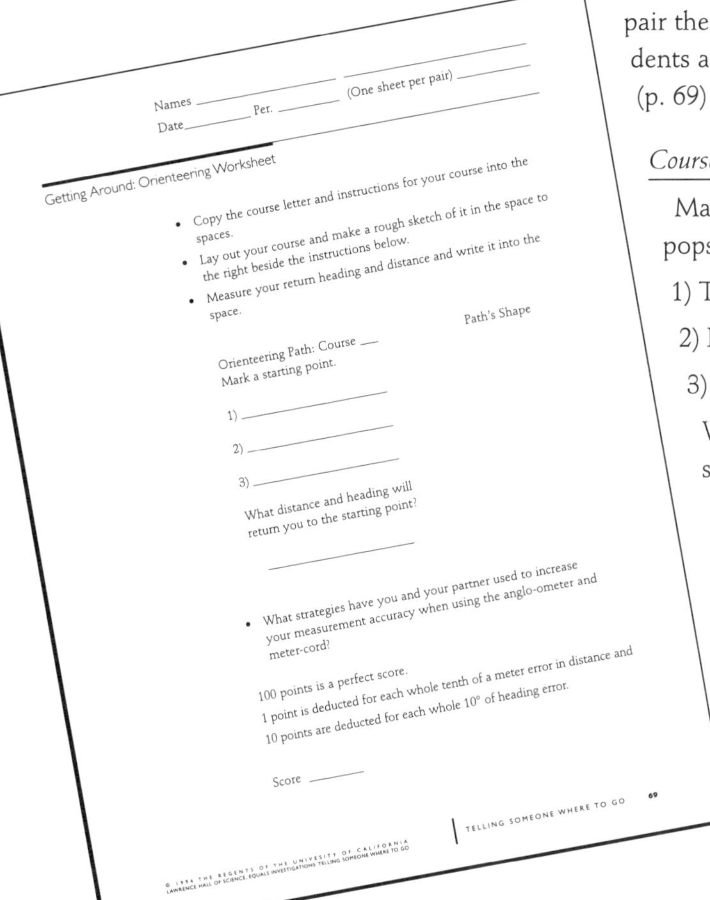

Names ______________________ (One sheet per pair) ______________

Date ________ Per. ________

Getting Around: Orienteering Worksheet

- Copy the course letter and instructions for your course into the spaces.
- Lay out your course and make a rough sketch of it in the space to the right beside the instructions below.
- Measure your return heading and distance and write it into the space.

Orienteering Path: Course __

Path's Shape

Mark a starting point.

1) ______________

2) ______________

3) ______________

What distance and heading will return you to the starting point?

____

- What strategies have you and your partner used to increase your measurement accuracy when using the anglo-ometer and meter-cord?

100 points is a perfect score.
1 point is deducted for each whole tenth of a meter error in distance and
10 points are deducted for each whole 10° of heading error.

Score ________

TELLING SOMEONE WHERE TO GO 69

Before sending students out to undertake different paths, pair them up to do *Course X*, below. Give each pair of students a copy of the *Getting Around: Orienteering Worksheet* (p. 69) and have them all fill in these instructions:

<u>*Course X*</u>

Mark your starting point with chalk (or a penny or a popsicle stick stake)

1) Turn 0°, go 4 meters
2) Left 90° and go 3.2 meters
3) Left 110° and go 4 meters

What is the heading and distance to return to your starting point?

(Actual measurements for the return: Left 62°, go 1.9 m.)

Take the class outside. Allow pairs to begin an *Orienteering Paths* for credit only after they have passed *Course X* with a score of 70 or better.

The *Orienteering Paths* sheet contains eight different courses. Print and cut up enough copies so each pair of students can be randomly assigned one course. Give each pair of students a copy of the *Getting Around: Orienteering (p. 69)* worksheet and one of the orienteering courses. Students should go outside and get to work. Those who finish early can try another orienteering course, but their score will be the average of the two, not the total. Answers for *Getting Around: Orienteering (p. 65)* outside courses are below. (Inside version answers are the same. Just multiply the distance numbers by ten and use cm as units.)

Answers:

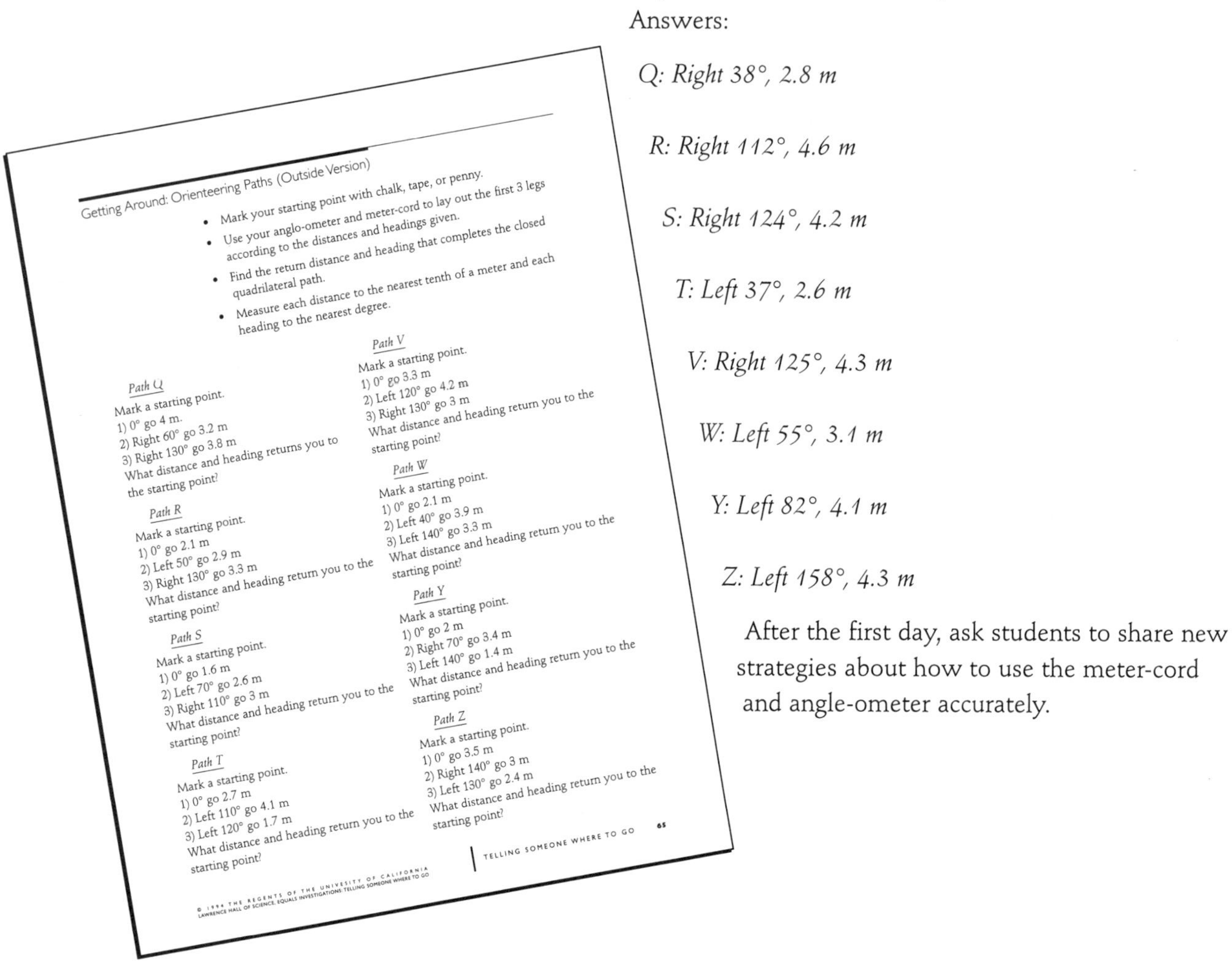

Getting Around: Orienteering Paths (Outside Version)

- Mark your starting point with chalk, tape, or penny.
- Use your anglo-ometer and meter-cord to lay out the first 3 legs according to the distances and headings given.
- Find the return distance and heading that completes the closed quadrilateral path.
- Measure each distance to the nearest tenth of a meter and each heading to the nearest degree.

Path Q
Mark a starting point.
1) 0° go 4 m.
2) Right 60° go 3.2 m
3) Right 130° go 3.8 m
What distance and heading returns you to the starting point?

Path R
Mark a starting point.
1) 0° go 2.1 m
2) Left 50° go 2.9 m
3) Right 130° go 3.3 m
What distance and heading return you to the starting point?

Path S
Mark a starting point.
1) 0° go 1.6 m
2) Left 70° go 2.6 m
3) Right 110° go 3 m
What distance and heading return you to the starting point?

Path T
Mark a starting point.
1) 0° go 2.7 m
2) Left 110° go 4.1 m
3) Left 120° go 1.7 m
What distance and heading return you to the starting point?

Path V
Mark a starting point.
1) 0° go 3.3 m
2) Left 120° go 4.2 m
3) Right 130° go 3 m
What distance and heading return you to the starting point?

Path W
Mark a starting point.
1) 0° go 2.1 m
2) Left 40° go 3.9 m
3) Left 140° go 3.3 m
What distance and heading return you to the starting point?

Path Y
Mark a starting point.
1) 0° go 2 m
2) Right 70° go 3.4 m
3) Left 140° go 1.4 m
What distance and heading return you to the starting point?

Path Z
Mark a starting point.
1) 0° go 3.5 m
2) Right 140° go 3 m
3) Left 130° go 2.4 m
What distance and heading return you to the starting point?

TELLING SOMEONE WHERE TO GO 65

© 1994 THE REGENTS OF THE UNIVERSITY OF CALIFORNIA. LAWRENCE HALL OF SCIENCE, EQUALS INVESTIGATIONS: TELLING SOMEONE WHERE TO GO

Q: Right 38°, 2.8 m

R: Right 112°, 4.6 m

S: Right 124°, 4.2 m

T: Left 37°, 2.6 m

V: Right 125°, 4.3 m

W: Left 55°, 3.1 m

Y: Left 82°, 4.1 m

Z: Left 158°, 4.3 m

After the first day, ask students to share new strategies about how to use the meter-cord and angle-ometer accurately.

■ HOMEWORK

Student paths created for problem 4 of *Walking Paths #2 (p. 61)* can be used as homework. Another idea is to take the students' statements on what must be true about the instructions for a rectangle and type them up into a true/false assignment. One statement should be written up and explained in detail.

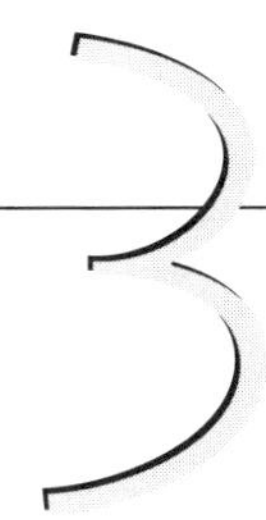

Orienteering On Paper With Protractors

In this task, students begin to work with rulers and protractors. Many students are unfamiliar with using a protractor to draw and measure angles. Their work in sessions 1 and 2 with the angle-ometer was preparation for understanding how to use the protractor.

- MATERIALS: *A protractor, centimeter ruler, and several sheets of unlined paper. For the teacher: a transparent protractor and centimeter ruler for overhead projector demonstration.*
- TIME: *1 hour*

Creating Closed Paths

COMPARING THE ANGLE-OMETER AND PROTRACTOR

Writing and discussion are essential in order for most students to transfer ideas from their work with the angle-ometer to the protractor. Each student needs a protractor and an angle-ometer. Ask the students to write about how the two instruments are alike and how they are different. Allow at least three minutes of silence for this writing. The comparison can take any form.

Ask for volunteers to read their writing aloud. The two scales at the edge of the typical protractor, one going from 0° to 180° and the other going from 180° down to 0°, are confusing for many students. In classes where this writing has been done, the discussion has led to the observation that the two sets of numbers on the protractor correspond to the numbers on the left-half and the right-half of the angle-ometer. One student noticed that "if two protractors are laid with their straight edges together, they make an angle-ometer." Another described the protractor as an "angle-ometer folded in half."

STUDENT GENERATED INSTRUCTIONS

There are no worksheets or transparencies for this task. Instead, each student needs a blank, unlined piece of paper, a protractor, and a centimeter ruler. The teacher needs an overhead transparency, a transparent protractor, and a centimeter ruler to demonstrate on the overhead projector.

In this task students will make accurate scale drawings of orienteering paths on 8.5" x 11" paper. Students will create paths for others to follow and also find the fourth leg on paths which other students have created.

Model Steps 1, 2, 3, and 4 for this task on the overhead. Let students know they are to make up their own paths as they follow along, not just copy your moves.

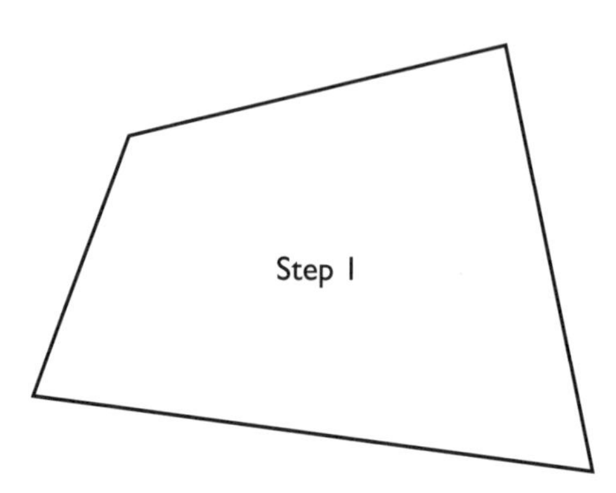

Draw a path

Use a ruler to draw a straight-line, closed path with four legs which is about hand-sized (takes up most of the paper but does not get too near the edges). Discourage use of rectangles and other "special" shapes. Above is a scaled-down sample shape.

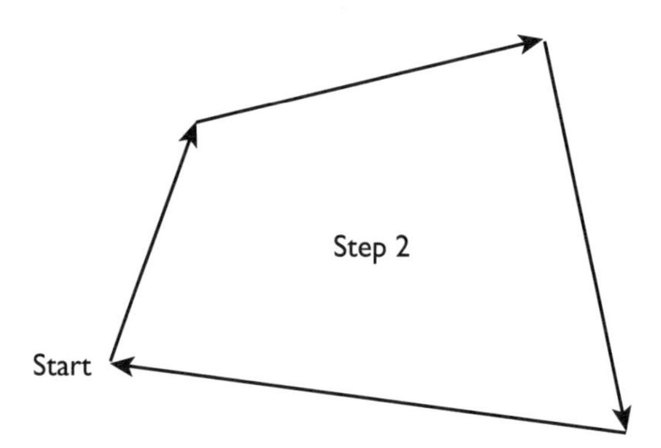

Label "Start" and direction

Imagine looking down upon a person walking along the four-legged, closed path. Label the "Start." Put arrow heads on the lines as shown to indicate the direction the person would walk along the path from start.

Measure distances

Measure the length of each leg to the nearest tenth of a centimeter.

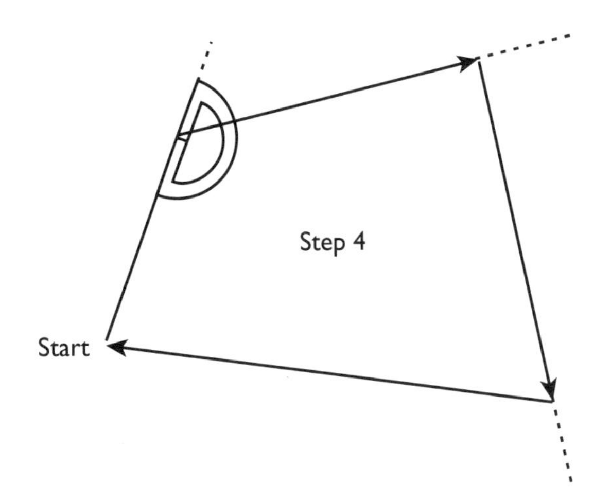

Measure headings

For headings, the same relative directional system (LOGO-style) is used for orienteering. Ask students to imagine walking their paths and to think about the turn they would have to make when walking the legs. Note: the heading of the first leg will always be 0°.

To measure the rest of the headings with a protractor, extend each arrow past the beginning of each next leg as shown above.

Use a transparent protractor on the overhead to demonstrate how to set the protractor along the path in order to measure the heading in degrees of a turn to the right or left. Some students will want to set the protractor with 90° straight ahead instead of 0°. Remind them that the protractor is like measuring with the right half or the left half of the angle-ometer and that the protractor must be positioned similarly to the diagram in order to measure correctly. Then ask students to measure the headings for their own paths. Have students check each other's distance and angle measurements for accuracy.

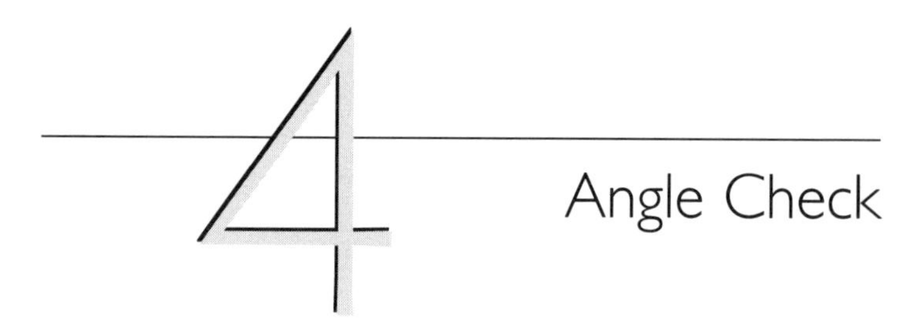

Angle Check

The idea underlying the Angle Check is that, if people walk around a closed path and finally face back in the direction they were facing at the start, then the total angle turned must be some multiple of 360°.

- MATERIALS: *Calculators*
- TIME: *1 hour*

The Angle Check

Before handing in the papers, have students add up the three angle headings for their path using a calculator in this way: clockwise turns are positive angles, and counter–clockwise turns are negative angles.

Since the turns in the diagram below are all clockwise, angle values are all positive.

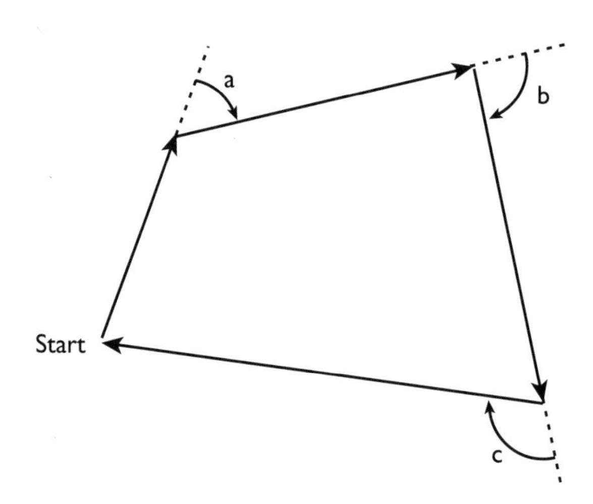

Suppose the headings labeled a, b, and c are Right 42°, Right 105°, and Right 126°.

On the calculator add 42° plus 105° plus 126°, for a total of 273°. This sum can be compared with the return angle labeled as return in the diagram below.

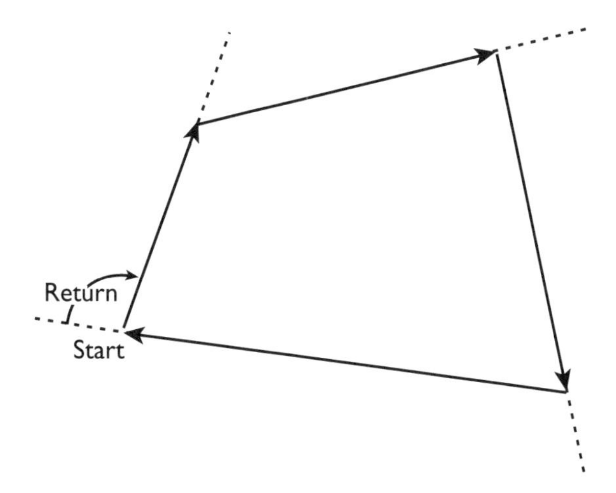

The return angle is the measurement of turn from the direction of the final leg in order to face in the direction of the first leg.

Since turning through all the headings plus the return angle gets a person facing in the direction they were originally pointing, this return angle for the diagram above is the amount that needs to be added to the above sum to make 360°. In the example above the return angle would have to be 360° minus 273°, or 87°.

In this way the return angle for a path can be measured with a protractor and compared with the calculated return angle for a check on overall accuracy of angle measurement.

■ WHAT IF THE TURNS ARE NOT ALL CLOCKWISE?

Clockwise turns are positive angles, and counter-clockwise turns are negative angles. Therefore, the angle sum including the return angle for any closed path should sum to either 360°, 0°, or -360°. In particular, for closed paths that cross back over themselves as in the bow-tie path below, the angle sum should be 0°.

Bow-tie Paths

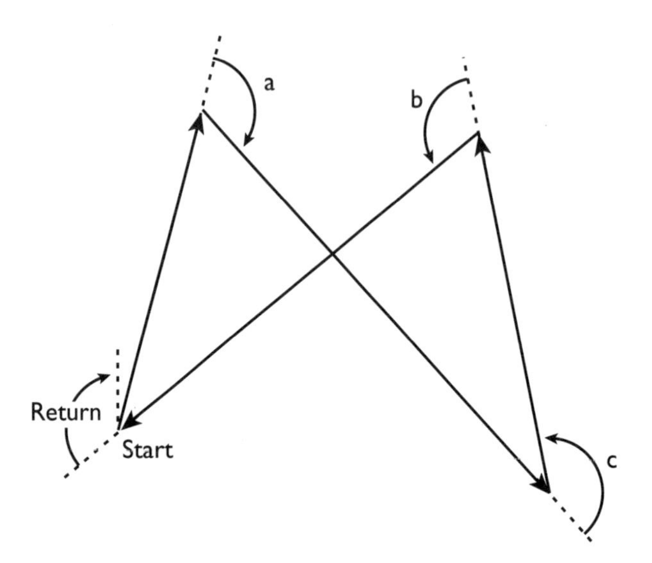

The two positive turns, labeled "a" and "return," will equal the opposite two negative turns, labeled "b" and "c," and so the four will equal 0°.

Concave or Boomerang Paths

For closed paths that are concave as in the diagram below, the angle sum should be 360°.

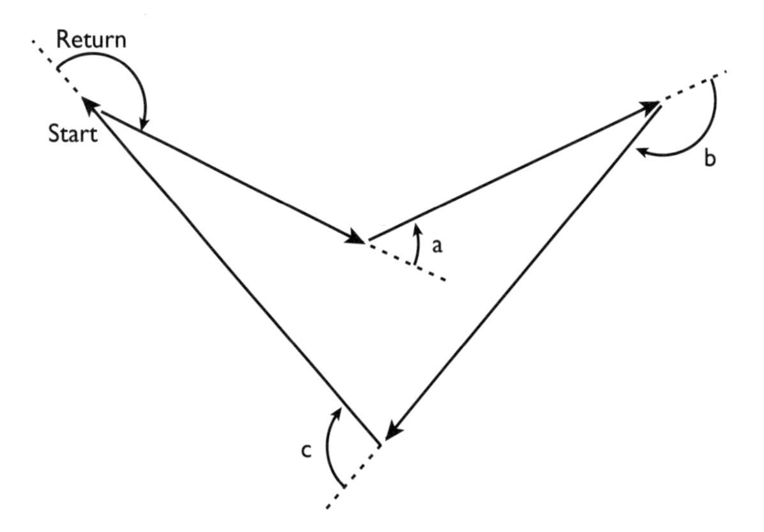

Finally, for paths traveled in a counterclockwise direction from "Start" and consisting mainly of left turns, the angle sum should come out to -360°.

■ PROCESSING THE SUMS OF THE ANGLES

A few students will raise questions about the validity of the class results on angle sums. Why should left turns be considered negative? Why can't they all be positive? How could bow-ties, after all that turning, be 0°? These are good and thoughtful questions. Turn it over to the groups for discussion. The questions that come up can be written on the overhead and copied for homework.

A teacher came up with a clever demonstration when one of his classes came to an impasse on the argument why bow-tie turns add up to 0°. He had a student hold one end of a meter-cord behind her, then someone else gave directions to have her walk a quadrilateral. The cord wrapped abound her. When they tried the same thing with instructions for a bow tie, she didn't get wrapped up.

■ USING STUDENT-DRAWN PATHS FOR ORIENTEERING PROBLEMS

Collect the student paths and select three that seem interesting and done correctly. Or, you may prefer to draw the paths accurately yourself. Copy the instructions only for the first three legs of each path on the board or overhead. Ask the students to copy the instructions for the three paths. Then students are to select any two of the three paths and draw the first three legs using a protractor and ruler, then measure to find the distance and heading for the fourth leg.

Scoring is the same as for the orienteering paths in section 2, except 1 point will be deducted for each 0.1 cm off, rather than for each 0.1 m off.

This entire session can be repeated another day, and used for homework periodically throughout the unit.

■ OPTIONAL INVESTIGATIONS

Bow Ties

What is the sum of the turn angles for multiple bow ties, such as those pictured below? Can the sums be generalized for the number of enclosed sections? For the number of intersections? For the number of legs?

 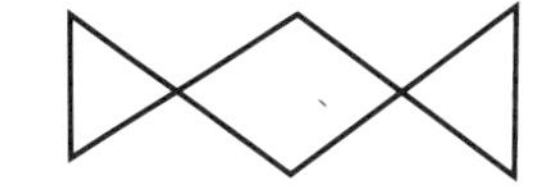 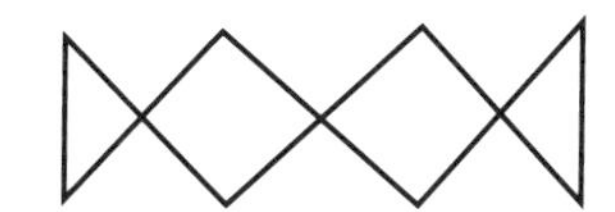

N-gons

What is the sum of the turn angles for paths shaped like polygons with 3, 4, 5...n sides? Can that pattern be generalized? (Yes. No matter how many sides, the turn angles always sum to 360°.)

Repeat Patterns

Give students the following instructions: Turn right 45°, go 3 cm. Repeat until you have a closed shape. What is the shape? (a regular octagon.) What other turn angles can be used in *repeat* instructions to make a closed path? Explore. Can all turn angles be used to make a closed path? Can you make a generalization about the turn angles that do? What other kinds of shapes are made? (stars.) This exploration would also be good for those with access to computers and LOGO.

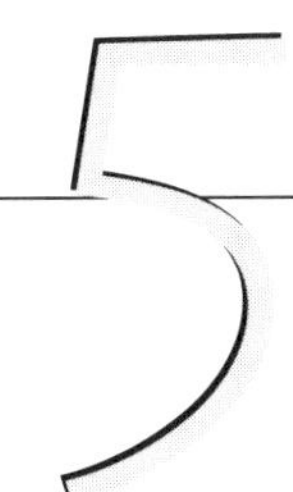

Navigating in the Dark (Optional)

In this session students will learn about the importance of accurate measurement in a real life application. The logistics of the *Navigating In the Dark* activity are complicated. But once students understand the sequence of events, the activity can be done over and over with different maps throughout the school year and provide a fun way to practice using the ruler and protractor with accuracy.

- MATERIALS: *Introduction Option 1, centimeter ruler, protractor* Demo Map *(p. 73),* Navigating Homework *(pp. 91, 93), Introduction Option 2, centimeter ruler, protractor, blank transparency, overhead pen,* Navigation Sheets (5) *(pp. 75–80), 4 copies of* Navigation Sheets *(pp. 75–80), 2* Navigational Masters Series *(p. 97),* Navigating in the Dark, Demo maps 1-5 *(pp. 81–90).*
4 or 5 business-sized envelopes, glue, scissors
transparencies: Demo Map *(p. 73),* Navigation Sheets (2) *(pp. 75–80),* Exxon Valdez Articles *(p. 71),*
Navigating in the Dark, maps 1-5 *(pp. 81–90),* Navigation in the Dark Instructions for the Investigation Reporter *(p. 95)*
Navigational Masters Series *(p. 97),* Homework *(pp. 91–93)*
transparent protractor, transparent centimeter ruler, overhead pen

- TIME: *2 hours*

Overview

First each group of students is given a set of maps. On each map islands and coastlines are drawn. The group must draw a route from "Here" to "There" on each map, safely avoiding the rocky shores. Then they measure and write the headings and distances for the routes on the outside of envelopes sealing the maps inside.

Next, the sealed envelopes are passed to another group. This group must use the instructions written on the outside of the envelope to draw the route "in the dark;" that is, on a blank map with "Here" and "There" marked, but with no islands or coastlines showing. They attach their routes drawn "in the dark" to the envelope.

Finally, the sealed envelope and routes drawn "in the dark" are passed to a third group. This group act as "investigative reporters." They open the sealed envelopes and place the maps drawn "in the dark" over the original maps showing the route and islands and hold them up so that light shines through. The "investigative reporters" then write a news story depending upon what they see: either the way the ship was safely maneuvered through the treacherous waters, or how the ship crashed into the rocky shores and why. If the ship crashes, it may be due to poorly written instructions (first group), or to errors in following instructions (second group), or both.

What follows are suggestions for introducing this activity to the class. However, you may want to use your own approach to get everyone started.

■ USING THE DEMO MAP TO INTRODUCE *NAVIGATING IN THE DARK*

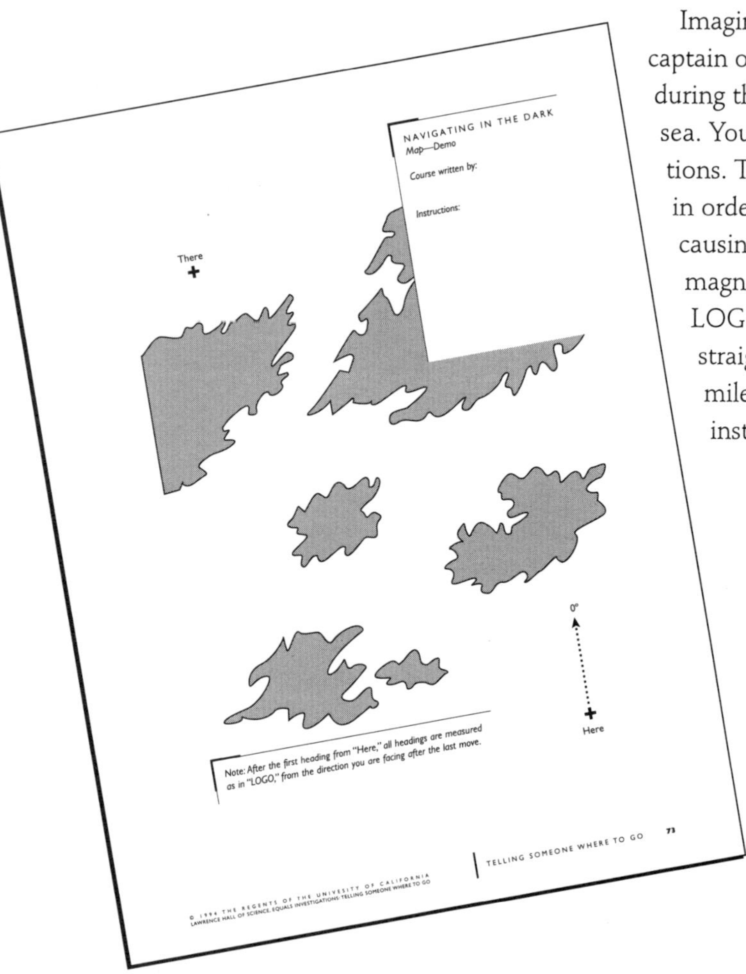

Imagine you have to give navigational directions to the captain of an oil tanker so that she can navigate her way during the night through a treacherous area of the Arctic sea. You have to give simple, precise, and safe instructions. The ship's captain has to follow them accurately in order to avoid crashing into the rocky shore and causing an environmental disaster. This far north your magnetic compass won't work, so you have to give LOGO-style heading instructions, where 0° is always straight ahead before turning. Distances will be in miles and the map scale will be 1 cm to 5 miles. All instructions will be written in centimeters.

The New York Times

NEW YORK, SATURDAY, MARCH 25, 1989

1 Largest U.S. Tanker Spill Spews Oil Off Alaska Coast

THE NEW YORK TIMES
THE ENVIRONMENT
TUESDAY, APRIL 4, 1989

Veterinarians and volunteers join to wash off the oil.

By Malcolm W. Browne

Special to the New York Times

Valdez, Alaska, April 3—Casualties by the hundreds are pouring into a makeshift hospital for oil-soaked animals here, where conditions have begun to resemble those in a battle-field aid situation.

The Valdez Bird and Animal Rescue Center was created on March 24, within hours after the tanker Exxon Valdez ran aground on a reef 14 miles south of here. Since then, three gashes in the tanker hull have poured about 10 million gallons of crude oil into Prince William Sound, killing or endangering great numbers of animals.

For more than a week after the accident, few animals injured by the oil spill were found or collected. But by last weekend the flood of victims began, and veterinarians were getting little sleep.

"This place is like a MASH unit at this point." Ms. Berkner said. "We have to work as fast as we can to stay ahead of the game."

2 Exxon Vessel Hits Reef, Fouling Water That Is Rich in Marine Life

By Philip Shabecoff

A tanker filled to capacity with crude oil ran aground and ruptured yesterday 25 miles from the southern end of the Trans Alaska Pipeline, spewing her cargo into water rich in marine life.

By evening the ship, the Exxon Valdez, had sent more than 270,000 barrels of oil into Prince William Sound, making this the largest tanker spill in United States history.

The New York Times/March 25, 1989

3 THE NEW YORK TIMES NATIONAL THURSDAY, FEBRUARY 15, 1990

Mate on Tanker Faults Helmsman in Accident

Second Day on Stand

This was the second day of Mr. Cousins's testimony in Anchorage Superior Court, where the 43-year-old Captain Hazelwood is standing trial on one felony count of second-degree criminal mischief and misdemeanor charges of reckless endangerment, negligent discharge of oil and operating a vessel while intoxicated. The maximum penalty for conviction on all counts is seven years, three months in prison and fines totaling $61,000.

The cross-examination was conducted by Dick Madson, who asked the witness, "Mr. Cousins, isn't it correct that in your mind there's no doubt that if that 10-degree right rudder had been executed, the ship would have cleared Bligh Reef by a substantial margin?"

Mr. Cousins described the night of the accident as extremely dark and misty. He said that about an hour before the grounding on the ship's radar screen he spotted ice in the channel. It was too dark to actually see the ice from the deck. Mr. Cousins said, but he reported it to Captain Hazelwood, who decided to divert the tanker from normal shipping lanes.

Mr. Cousins and a helmsman, Robert Kagan, were at the wheel when the 987-foot tanker ran aground, spilling nearly 11 million gallons of crude oil in the nation's worst oil spill.

Grounding Interrupts Call

Mr. Cousins said that before he called he began to believe that Mr. Kagan was not properly following his orders to make a sharp change in the ship's course. never worked with Mr. Kagan before and had heard rumors the seaman had problems with steering on another voyage.

The testimony came in the cross-examination by Captain Hazelwood's lawyer, who sought to show that all the procedures aboard the tanker were moving smoothly until the helmsman failed to execute a 10-degree right turn.

Mr. Cousins, who was told by Captain Hazelwood to take command of the tanker about 10 minutes before it went aground, suggested that Mr. Kagan caused the spill by not following orders to turn the wheel hard.

He said he was convinced that had the helmsman followed orders, the ship would have missed by several miles the rocky reef that she ultimately hit.

…E TO GO 71

NAVIGATING IN THE DARK
Map—

Course written by:

Course navigated by:

Instructions:

There +

0°

+ Here

Note: After the first heading from "Here," all headings are measured as in "LOGO," from the direction you are facing after the last move.

TELLING SOMEONE WHERE TO GO 75

© 1994 THE REGENTS OF THE UNIVERSITY OF CALIFORNIA
LAWRENCE HALL OF SCIENCE, EQUALS INVESTIGATIONS: TELLING SOMEONE WHERE TO GO

To emphasize the necessity of these skills, news clippings about the devastation caused by the 1989 crash and oil spill of the Exxon Valdez have been included for class discussion. Share a transparency of the clippings. The third article especially points out the importance of measurement; testimony of the Exxon Valdez' captain focused on the helmsman's inability to make a full 10° turn.

To introduce *Navigating in the Dark* you may choose Option 1 or Option 2. Option 1 involves sending two students out of the room and then having everyone watch them as they try to follow a path devised by another student on the overhead. Option 2 has all students try to draw two given paths without knowing where islands are, and then having each student self-assess how well the instructions were followed.

■ INTRODUCTION—OPTION I

Prepare an overhead transparency of the *Demo Map* (p. 73) and two transparencies of the blank *Navigation Sheet* (p. 75). Send two brave students out of the room so they will be "in the dark" about the details of the map. You may want to arrange a place for them to be for 5 to 15 minutes.

Have students work in pairs. Give each pair a paper copy of the *Demo Map,* protractors, and centimeter rulers. Each pair is to draw a path from "Here" to "There." No curves allowed; legs of all paths are to be straight lines.

Use the transparency of the *Demo Map* to show students that they should start their paths at the plus sign and not on the end of the arrow head. You may want to show how you would draw and measure your first leg, but let them know they may choose any initial direction they want.

After they draw their paths, they write distance and heading instructions using centimeters and

LOGO-style headings. Have two of the pairs who are done early copy their instructions into the box on the transparency of a blank *Navigation Sheet.*

Call the two students back into the room. Have one student come up to the overhead. Put one of the blank *Navigation Sheet* transparencies on the overhead. Give the student an overhead pen, a transparent protractor, and a transparent cm ruler to draw the path. No information other than the written instructions should be given. Repeat with another pair's instructions and the other brave student. Then place the transparency of the map over the two paths to see if either student made it from "Here" to "There" without crashing into the coastlines.

■ INTRODUCTION—OPTION 2

The following instructions are for two different paths through the *Demo Map*.

Course 1:

1) Turn right 20°, go 8.4 cm
2) Turn left 20°, go 3.0 cm
3) Turn left 87°, go 11.5 cm
4) Turn right 112°, go 7.6 cm
5) Turn left 103°, go 4.3 cm

Course 2:

1) Turn left 49°, go 8.5 cm
2) Turn left 27°, go 6.9 cm
3) Turn right 117°, go 11.9 cm
4) Turn left 123°, go 5.9 cm

Pass out two blank *Navigation Sheets,* a centimeter ruler, and a protractor to each student, or each pair of students. Have them write in "Demo," and copy the instructions in the box. Have students follow the directions and draw the path.

You may give a transparency to some students to copy their paths onto. Later, when most students have completed their paths, these transparencies can be placed on the overhead over the *Demo Map* transparency to see if they navigated safely.

One copy of the *Demo Map* can be given to each group as they finish. Students should check that their ships did not crash by placing the map behind their *Navigation Sheet* and holding both up to the light.

Navigating In The Dark

■ WRITING DIRECTIONS

Provide each group with four business-sized envelopes, four blank *Navigation Sheets* (p. 75), two *Navigational Masters* (p. 97) record sheets, glue and scissors, and a set of *Navigating in the Dark* maps (p. 81). (Use four of the maps; five maps are included in the set. Use the fifth map for groups of five, or save it for later in the year.) Ask students to check each other's work. When a student completes a map and instruction sheet, another member of the group should check the instructions and measurements for accuracy. Then the map-maker should place the map inside the envelope, glue the instruction sheet to the outside of the envelope, and seal it. Give students enough time so that you are sure everyone has completed one map and envelope.

■ FOLLOWING DIRECTIONS

The next day you can pass out the envelopes so each group gets instructions for paths through unknown waters. One method is to pass group 1's to group 2, group 2's to group 3, and so on until each group has another group's work. If you teach more than one math class, 1st period's papers could go to 2nd period, and so on. Pass out two or three blank *Navigation Sheets* to each student. Students should then follow the instructions on the outside of the envelopes, plotting the course from "Here" to "There" as accurately as they can. They should not open the envelope, but should sign on the outside indicating that they have completed that particular set of instructions.

After finishing one envelope, the student may go on to another. Wait until everyone has had a chance to follow at least one set of instructions before checking paths for accuracy.

Instructions for the Investigative Reporter

1. Place the Navigation Sheet over the original map to find any errors.
2. If there are places where the paths don't match, mark them and circle the instructions that match them.
3. Check all the measurements yourself to see where errors, if any, occurred.
4. Write a brief article reporting your findings. Tell exactly where the errors occurred. Be sensitive to and respectful of the novice course writers and captains.
5. Attach your article to the map and the Navigation sheets and return them to your teacher.

TELLING SOMEONE WHERE TO GO 95

Map—2

Course written by:

Instructions:

There

0°

Here

Note: After the first heading from "Here," all headings are measured as in "LOGO," from the direction you are facing after the last move.

TELLING SOMEONE WHERE TO GO 83

Pass the envelopes containing the maps and the *Navigation Sheets* to a third group. They will act as Investigative News Reporters to determine if there were errors made and who made them. If there were any accidents at sea, they are to discover and report on where and why the accidents occurred. Whatever they discover should be written up in a journalistic style. Encourage these budding journalists not to make derogatory comments, and to treat those they write about with respect.

Put the transparency *Instructions for the Investigative Reporter* (p. 95) up on the overhead. The reports students write should address each item. Once the report has been written, the *Navigation Sheets* and maps should be returned to their respective envelopes. By the end of the period, all envelopes should be returned to the students who made up the navigational courses so that they can read them and see how they did.

■ INTRODUCING THE INVESTIGATIVE REPORTER TASK

Worksheets are provided for two items: a sample Map 2 with path drawn, but incorrect instructions written, and a matching *Navigation Sheet* with the incorrect instructions followed. These items can be used to illustrate the Investigative Reporter task to students. Or you may draw your own map and *Navigation Sheet* with errors. On the sample path, the third leg of the instructions should be left 110° instead of 115°. The fourth leg should be 8.3 cm, not 7.3 cm. On the *Navigation Sheet* the instructions were followed correctly as they were written. The errors in this case were due to faulty instructions.

Point out to students that, in other cases, the instructions may be correct, but the person drawing the path from the instructions may have made an error.

Show how to compare each pair of corresponding lengths on the maps by superimposing the two maps and then moving the top transparency to match, in turn, each individual distance. Since, in the sample

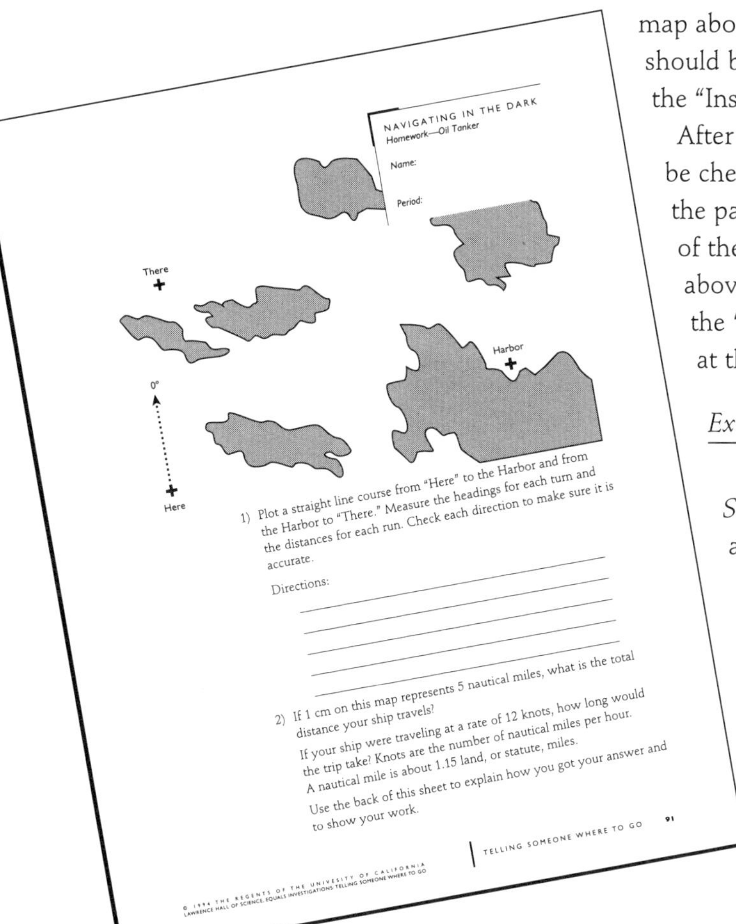
NAVIGATING IN THE DARK
Homework—Oil Tanker

Name:

Period:

1) Plot a straight line course from "Here" to the Harbor and from the Harbor to "There." Measure the headings for each turn and the distances for each run. Check each direction to make sure it is accurate.

Directions:

2) If 1 cm on this map represents 5 nautical miles, what is the total distance your ship travels?

If your ship were traveling at a rate of 12 knots, how long would the trip take? Knots are the number of nautical miles per hour. A nautical mile is about 1.15 land, or statute, miles.

Use the back of this sheet to explain how you got your answer and to show your work.

map above, only one of the lengths was off, this error should be mentioned in the "news report" and circled in the "Instructions Box" on the map.

After comparing lengths, the heading angles need to be checked in a similar fashion. The turns on each of the paths can be compared by superimposing the legs of the paths before and after each turn. In the sample above, the one erroneous turn would be described in the "news report" and circled on the *Navigation Sheet* at the site of the error and in the Instructions box.

Extension

Students may enjoy using the blank *Navigation Sheets* (p. 75) to create their own maps with hazards of their own design.

■ HOMEWORK

Two worksheets have been included which may be used as homework.

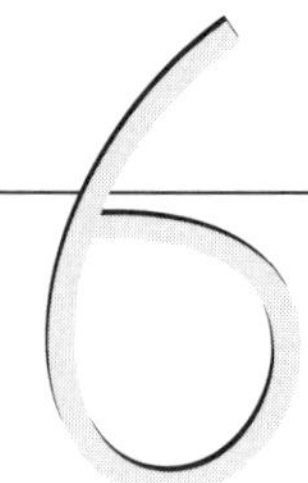

Changes in Paths Resulting From Changes In Lengths

In this session students begin some exploratory investigations to discover what *happens* to a path when the lengths of its legs are changed. The two changes that will be explored are **adding the same length** to each leg, and **multiplying each leg** by the same quantity.

When relatively small numbers are added to lengths, or numbers close to one are used to multiply lengths, the changes in the shape of the path are difficult to see. So a new test for similarity, the **Ratio Check**, is introduced to students.

- MATERIALS: *A protractor, centimeter ruler, and calculator; transparency of:* Changes in Paths Resulting From Changes in Lengths *(p. 99).*
- TIME: *2 hours*

Name ______________________

Changes in Paths Resulting From Changes In Lengths

When navigation equipment is faulty or measurement tools are not precise, errors are compounded, especially when a path consists of several legs. To analyze errors, it is important to know how changes in directions affect paths navigated.

We will analyze the effects of two kinds of changes, adding and multiplying:

1. How does a path change if the length of each leg has some distance, such as 1.5 cm, added?

2. How does a path change if the length of each leg is multiplied by some number, such as 1.5?

Your assignment:

- Choose a four-legged path to be your original.
- Make the changes suggested in questions 1 and 2 and draw the new figures.
- Write up your findings, using your drawings and Ratio Checks as evidence.

Introducing the Investigation

Boomerang-type paths from session 3 with four unequal legs work especially well to illustrate the difference between enlarging by adding and multiplying. Post the instructions for the first three legs. Have the students copy the instructions for the path, draw the figure, and find the heading and direction for the fourth leg. Discuss the results; everyone should have nearly the same diagrams and nearly the same values for heading and direction.

Share the transparency *Changes in Paths Resulting From Changes in Lengths* (p. 99). Ask students to discuss what they predict will happen in each case. Have them sketch and write what they think will happen with each kind of alteration. Which one will be bigger? Will they both have the same shape as the original figure (be mathematically similar)? Will closed paths remain closed?

It may be helpful to brainstorm with the class what similar and congruent mean. Encourage them to give examples.

After they have written their hypotheses, ask the students to share their ideas. Then have them draw the new paths resulting from the new instructions. How do their results compare with their hypothesis?

■ RATIO CHECK

Ask students if their conclusions about the effects of adding and multiplying are true for any original path. In life, many people make generalizations based on a single experience, but in mathematics, exploring one case is not enough. To make a generalization, a mathematician explores many cases, and finally uses his/her experience to explain why a generalization must be true (or false). Drawing many diagrams is an important way for a mathematician to learn about a situation. The **Ratio Check**, a mathematical tool involving numbers, can be helpful when testing various cases.

Below is a sample path that will be used to illustrate enlarging by adding, by multiplying and the idea of the **Ratio Check**.

Write the instructions for this path and have students draw the path.

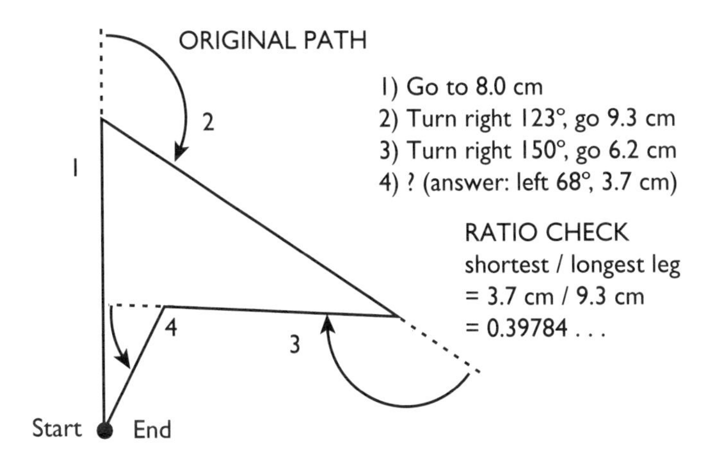

Have students calculate the ratio of the shortest to the longest leg of this path. There is no special reason for using the ratio shortest to longest. When comparing ratios, the sides used in the ratio need only be corresponding sides. The same two sides must be used in the original and new figures. Shortest to longest is chosen for convenience. In this case 3.7 to 9.3 reduces to 0.397849... or 0.40.

Next have students add 1.5 cm to each leg of this path and draw the resulting new path. If 1.5 cm were added to each leg, the resulting path would be as follows:

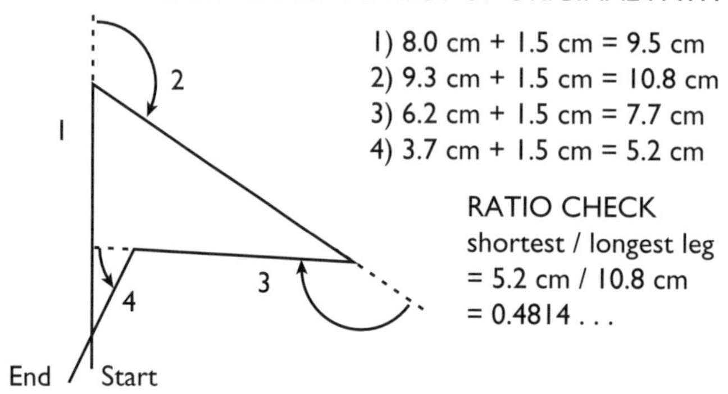

Ask students to point out how this shape compares to the original. Are the shapes the same? Is the path still closed? How are they different?

Have students calculate the ratio of the shortest to longest leg. In this case the ratio 5.2/10.8 reduces to 0.4814. . . . Adding 1.5 cm to each leg of a concave quadrilateral creates a larger figure, but the ratio for the new shape is different. Thus the shape is not similar to the original.

In this case the shapes are visibly different. Even if there were no visible difference, the **Ratio Check** shows that the new shape is not similar to the original one.

The temptation to simply connect the final leg to make it turn out "right" is too great for some students. Discuss the dangers of fudging the results of experiments. If they were scientists, and fudged their results, they could obscure important discoveries.

Ask students if it makes sense to use the **Angle Check** on a path that is not closed. Discussion should result in a "no". The **Angle Check** works only on closed paths with a return angle.

Now have students multiply each length of the original by 1.5 and draw the resulting shape.

When the length of each leg is multiplied by 1.5, the result is as follows (not drawn to precise scale):

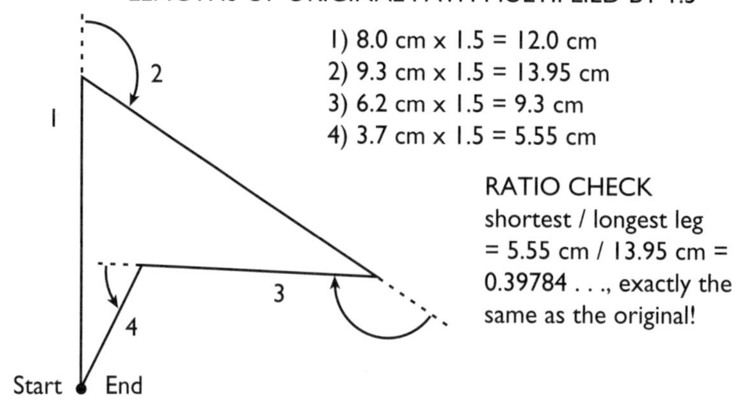

The endpoints of the path match, and the figure appears to have the same shape as the original. The ratio of the shortest to longest leg is 5.55 to 13.95, or 0.39784. . ., which is exactly the same as the original. The ratio of the corresponding lengths must be the same for the figures to be similar. Enlarging a quadrilateral by multiplying the length of each leg by the same factor creates a similar figure.

■ HOMEWORK

For homework, students should try another case. Have them select a number other than 1.5. Ask them to use the original concave path to **add to**, and **multiply by** the leg lengths. Draw the modified path, and use the **Ratio Check** with one of the adjacent sides to verify similarity. Have the students repeat the same thing after multiplying each leg by their new number. Encourage them to avoid "whole-number-itis," and choose non-whole numbers.

* *The investigation will be continued during the* Group Investigation project *in session 7.*

■ STUDENT UNDERSTANDING OF THE RATIO CHECK

At this point, many students may not understand the usefulness of the **Ratio Check** and when were asked to share their understanding they gave a variety of responses including:

- It's the ratio of the circle, but different. In a rectangle it's the same, but here we have to know the length.
- We did this to find out if it equaled 360°. If we divided the longest by the shortest it wouldn't work.
- We did the **Ratio Check** because we wanted to see what is the answer.
- We used it to find the level of accuracy by comparing sizes. Example: short to long = 5 to 10 = 0.5. If you multiply by 5 the shape gets 5 times bigger. Then short to long = 25 to 50 = 0.5.
- We did the **Ratio Check** because we can find out if they are the same.
- So you will know the decimal. You will know how much larger the picture is.

Do not despair. Continue to ask them to find and compare the ratios. Eventually, some students will get a better understanding of proportionality. It is a difficult concept and takes time to understand fully. It is not essential to "master" this concept to be successful in this unit.

7 Group Investigation Project

What Happens To Paths When Leg Lengths Are Changed?

In this session, the investigation begun in session 5 is continued. To accumulate more evidence, each group will be assigned a different kind of path to investigate. Each group will make an oral presentation of their findings to the class. During the presentations, students will need to take notes to use as a reference while working on their Individual Projects in session 8.

■ MATERIALS: *Poster paper or transparencies, pens, rulers, protractors, calculators; student worksheets:* Mathematics Toolkit *(p. 101)*, Group Investigation Assignment *(p. 105)*, Paths For Group Investigations *(p. 103)*, Step-by-Step Guide For Doing the Group Investigation-optional *(p. 107)*; *transparencies of:* Group Investigation Assignment *(p. 105)*, Paths For Group Investigations *(p. 103)*.

■ TIME: *3 hours*

Each group will investigate the same three questions listed below, using different original shapes:

- What happens to the shape of all paths when you add the same length to each leg?
- What happens to the shape of all paths when you multiply each leg by the same number?
- Are there particular paths, or special numbers, that are exceptions?

Eight different kinds of path shapes are provided, enough so each group in a class can explore a different path shape. For classes with more than eight groups, two groups can be assigned the same path type.

Names of group members:

Group Investigation Assignment

Path shape your group is assigned:

As a group, research and prepare an oral report for the class about your shape. Include answers to the three questions below.

What happens to any path if the same number is added to (or subtracted from) the length of each leg? Why?

What happens to any path if each leg of the path is multiplied or divided by the same number? Why?

Are there any kinds of paths that are exceptions to your findings? Your report must include several accurate drawings as evidence to support your answers.

After all reports are complete, the class will compile the information and try to answer the three questions for paths of all shapes.

TELLING SOMEONE WHERE TO GO 105

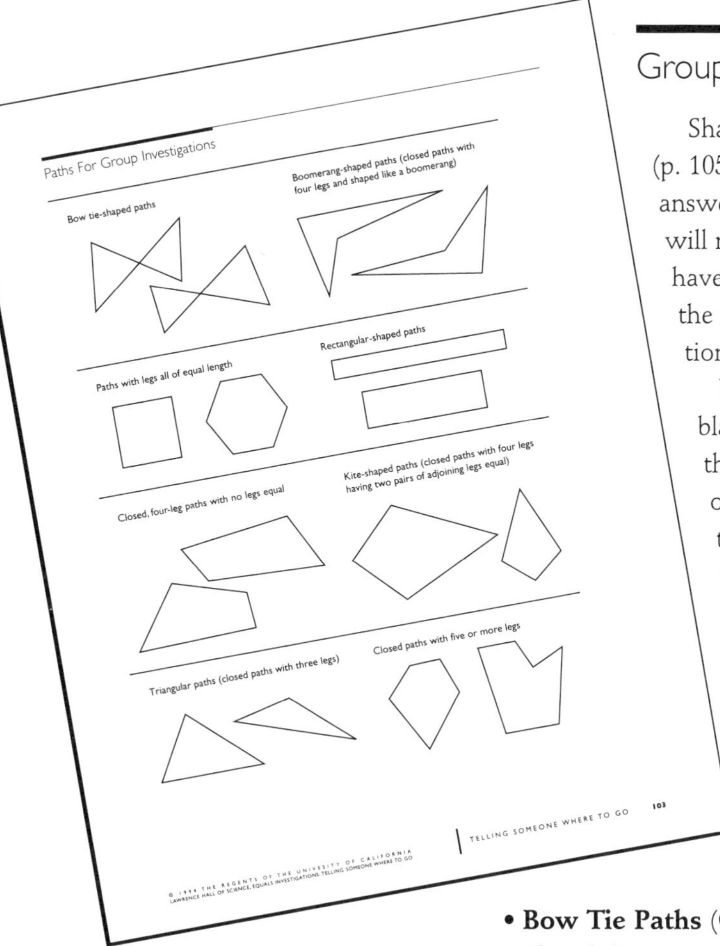
Paths For Group Investigations

Bow tie-shaped paths

Boomerang-shaped paths (closed paths with four legs and shaped like a boomerang)

Paths with legs all of equal length

Rectangular-shaped paths

Closed, four-leg paths with no legs equal

Kite-shaped paths (closed paths with four legs having two pairs of adjoining legs equal)

Triangular paths (closed paths with three legs)

Closed paths with five or more legs

TELLING SOMEONE WHERE TO GO 103

© 1994 THE REGENTS OF THE UNIVERSITY OF CALIFORNIA
LAWRENCE HALL OF SCIENCE, EQUALS INVESTIGATIONS: TELLING SOMEONE WHERE TO GO

Group Investigation Assignment

Share the transparency *Group Investigation Assignment* (p. 105) with the class. Emphasize that all groups will answer the same three questions although each group will research a different kind of path. Each group will have to be clear when reporting to the class, because all the other groups will be relying on them for information and evidence to make generalizations.

Each group of four students needs chart paper or blank transparencies and pens. Allow at least two or three class periods (minimum 2 hours with an overnight) to complete the investigation. Encourage the groups to sketch their diagrams and test their ideas before drawing their posters or transparencies.

Share the transparency *Paths For Group Investigations* (p. 103).

In a random way, assign one kind of path shape to each group.

For your information, here are brief descriptions of each kind of path shape along with some suggestions:

- **Bow Tie Paths** (Closed paths with four legs having the second and fourth legs cross each other.)
- **Boomerang Paths** (Closed paths with four legs that are shaped like boomerangs.)
- **Paths With All Legs of Equal Length** Altering lengths by addition or multiplication result in shapes similar to this kind of original path. This task is appropriate for a group that has already gained a thorough grasp of the differences between altering by addition and by multiplication.
- **Rectangular Paths** Distortion of rectangles is harder to recognize and requires using the **Ratio Check** to verify distortion. The endpoints always meet. This task is appropriate to a group that already understands the differences between altering by addition and by multiplication on less symmetrical paths.
- **Closed, Four-leg Paths With No Legs Equal**
- **Kite Paths** (Closed paths with four legs having two pairs of congruent adjoining legs.)
- **Triangular Paths** (Closed paths with three legs.) The effects are often more evident on triangles, so you may wish to assign this task to a group that needs to see clear conclusions.
- **Closed Paths With Five Or More Legs**

If some groups have a hard time getting started, you may give them a copy of the *Step-by-Step Guide For Group Investigation* (p. 107).

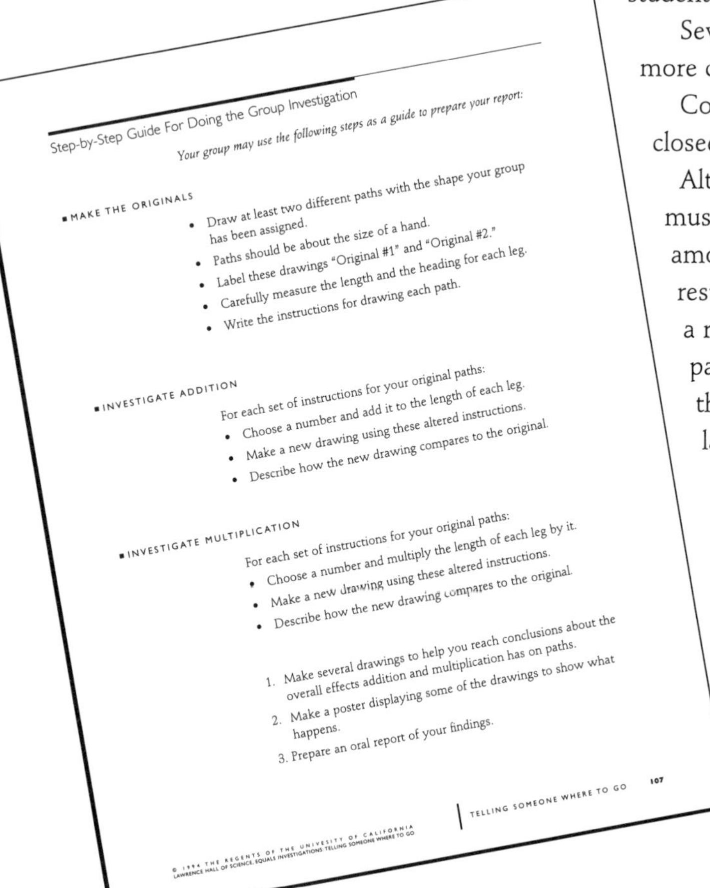

Step-by-Step Guide For Doing the Group Investigation

Your group may use the following steps as a guide to prepare your report:

■ MAKE THE ORIGINALS

- Draw at least two different paths with the shape your group has been assigned.
- Paths should be about the size of a hand.
- Label these drawings "Original #1" and "Original #2."
- Carefully measure the length and the heading for each leg.
- Write the instructions for drawing each path.

■ INVESTIGATE ADDITION

For each set of instructions for your original paths:

- Choose a number and add it to the length of each leg.
- Make a new drawing using these altered instructions.
- Describe how the new drawing compares to the original.

■ INVESTIGATE MULTIPLICATION

For each set of instructions for your original paths:

- Choose a number and multiply the length of each leg by it.
- Make a new drawing using these altered instructions.
- Describe how the new drawing compares to the original.

1. Make several drawings to help you reach conclusions about the overall effects addition and multiplication has on paths.
2. Make a poster displaying some of the drawings to show what happens.
3. Prepare an oral report of your findings.

TELLING SOMEONE WHERE TO GO 107

© 1994 THE REGENTS OF THE UNIVERSITY OF CALIFORNIA
LAWRENCE HALL OF SCIENCE, EQUALS INVESTIGATIONS: TELLING SOMEONE WHERE TO GO

While the groups are working, here are some things for the students to remember:

Several paths need to be drawn and investigated to be more certain about conclusions.

Conduct **Angle Checks** if the path they are exploring is closed.

Although similar figures may be different sizes, they must have exactly the same shape. Adding the same amount to each leg for some shapes, such as squares, will result in a shape that is similar to the original. However, a relatively small number added to each leg of some paths may cause its shape to appear unchanged. In these cases, the **Ratio Check** is useful to test for similarity.

A discussion of the mathematical technique called "consider extreme cases" may help groups decide what numbers to use. What would happen if you added a very small number to each length, versus a very large number?

Instead of drawing, some groups may find it easier to pace out paths to see what happens. They can make up instructions for a simple path and pace it out with the lengths doubled, or with 3 more paces added to each leg.

■ THE POSTER

Explain to all groups that their posters will be visual aids displaying some of their work for their oral report. You may discuss and post the following poster guidelines:

- Make it easy to read from a distance.
- Use a title relating to the problem.
- Include a few diagrams that best illustrate the results of the research.
- Include a brief summary of the conclusions.

■ MATHEMATICS TOOLKIT AND GROUP INVESTIGATIONS RESULTS

Before the group reports begin, pass out a copy of the *Mathematics Toolkit* (p. 101) to each student. They can write notes on what they learn from other groups presentations.

Remind students that the *Toolkit* is NOT an assessment. It is being used to clarify some of the complicated ideas encountered. They may find the *Toolkit* a useful reference when working on their own individual project.

Have students write their own ideas for **Angle Check, Similar Shapes** and **Ratio Check**. Ask some students to share what they have written with the class. Verbally sharing their ideas will help others to express their ideas in words. Paraphrasing and asking clarifying questions can help students express themselves.

Name

Mathematics Toolkit

In your own words, write a definition for each term below and describe why it is useful. Give at least one example and include a sketch for each term:

■ ANGLE CHECK

■ SIMILAR SHAPES

■ RATIO CHECK

Based on the Group Reports, what can you say about changes in paths when:

1) all legs of the original path have the same length added to them?

2) all legs of the original path are multiplied by the same number?

© 1994 THE REGENTS OF THE UNIVERSITY OF CALIFORNIA
LAWRENCE HALL OF SCIENCE, EQUALS INVESTIGATIONS: TELLING SOMEONE WHERE TO GO

TELLING SOMEONE WHERE TO GO 101

■ GROUP REPORTS

Each group should make an oral report to the rest of the class. Randomly choose which group will report first. Do not allow groups to continue working while others are reporting. Allow each group a set amount of time, such as 5 minutes for reporting.

During the reporting, limit your own and other student comments to paraphrasing what groups have said or to asking questions for clarification of a group's statement. Refrain from discussing "right" or "wrong" or from pointing out errors until all groups have reported. Corrections in faulty thinking are much more effective if done by peers. Group papers or transparencies can be posted on the walls and referred to during the individual project work time.

You may want to post the following oral presentation guidelines for groups to use:

- Everyone must present.
- Explain the problem so that anyone can understand it.
- Describe the experiments conducted.
- Tell how your group shared the responsibilities.
- Share your conclusions.
- Discuss problems you had and questions still remaining. Ask for class input for any questions you did not solve.

■ REVISITING THE MATHEMATICS TOOLKIT

✱ What if students present erroneous ideas during the discussion? Encourage them to challenge points with counter-examples. A counter example is a case for which the erroneous idea does not work. If a student says something that you know is wrong and no one in the class can correct the idea, then it becomes your job to give the class a counterexample to investigate for homework.

After the group reports are complete, have a class discussion about questions 1 and 2 at the bottom of the *Toolkit* page. To ensure that no group agrees on something erroneous and enters it into their *Toolkit* as fact, you may want to have students wait until the conclusion of the class discussion to write their responses to questions 1 and 2.

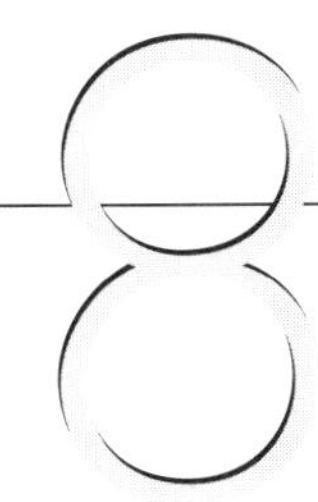

Individual Project

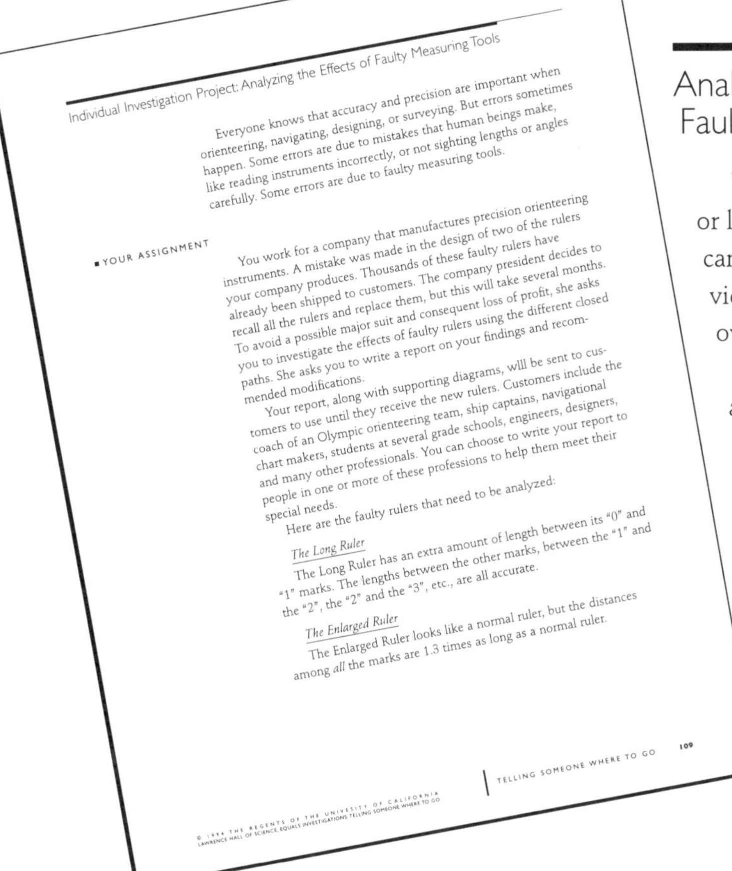

Individual Investigation Project: Analyzing the Effects of Faulty Measuring Tools

Everyone knows that accuracy and precision are important when orienteering, navigating, designing, or surveying. But errors sometimes happen. Some errors are due to mistakes that human beings make, like reading instruments incorrectly, or not sighting lengths or angles carefully. Some errors are due to faulty measuring tools.

■ YOUR ASSIGNMENT

You work for a company that manufactures precision orienteering instruments. A mistake was made in the design of two of the rulers your company produces. Thousands of these faulty rulers have already been shipped to customers. The company president decides to recall all the rulers and replace them, but this will take several months. To avoid a possible major suit and consequent loss of profit, she asks you to investigate the effects of faulty rulers using the different closed paths. She asks you to write a report on your findings and recommended modifications.

Your report, along with supporting diagrams, wlll be sent to customers to use until they receive the new rulers. Customers include the coach of an Olympic orienteering team, ship captains, navigational chart makers, students at several grade schools, engineers, designers, and many other professionals. You can choose to write your report to people in one or more of these professions to help them meet their special needs.

Here are the faulty rulers that need to be analyzed:

The Long Ruler

The Long Ruler has an extra amount of length between its "0" and "1" marks. The lengths between the other marks, between the "1" and the "2", the "2" and the "3", etc., are all accurate.

The Enlarged Ruler

The Enlarged Ruler looks like a normal ruler, but the distances among *all* the marks are 1.3 times as long as a normal ruler.

TELLING SOMEONE WHERE TO GO 109

© 1994 THE REGENTS OF THE UNIVESITY OF CALIFORNIA
LAWRENCE HALL OF SCIENCE, EQUALS INVESTIGATIONS: TELLING SOMEONE WHERE TO GO

Analyzing the Effects of Faulty Measuring Tools

Work on the individual project may last a week or longer and involve several revisions. Peer editing can be used. Students may collaborate on the individual project, but each student should hand in her own project.

The assignment for the individual project is an extension and personalization of the group research project. Explorations begun in the group project can be completed or extended in order to research the effect of using faulty measuring tools.

■ **MATERIALS:** *Student worksheets:* Individual Project: Analyzing the Effects of Faulty Measuring Tools *(p. 109)* Individual Project Self-Evaluation *(p. 111).*

■ **TIME:** *5 hours*

■ SUGGESTIONS FOR GETTING STUDENTS STARTED

The instructions for the *Individual Investigation* (p. 109) are "open" in the sense that specific questions to be answered are not given, nor is a particular method for organizing work specified. For some students this openness causes anxiety, especially if they have not had much experience in doing individual investigations in math.

You may provide more structure for the assignment if you feel your students need it. You may chose to require a table of contents, a certain set of diagrams, a log of work done each day, or a series of deadlines to be met for each part of the project. You may ask students to narrow the focus of the investigation to initially include only four-sided paths or triangles.

Names ______________ Period ______________
Date ______________

Individual Investigation Self-Evaluation

The individual investigation is your opportunity to show what you have learned in this unit. Check the spaces as you complete them.

▪ DIAGRAMS OF FAULTY TOOLS:
Long Ruler ______________ ____
Enlarged Ruler ______________ ____

▪ A VARIETY OF CLOSED PATHS (CIRCLE AT LEAST FOUR SHAPES):
Square Rectangle Rhombus Trapezoid "Bow-tie"
Four unequal legs Boomerang Parallelogram
Other______

How many diagrams did you use to show what happens for each tool?:
Regular Ruler____ Long Ruler____ Enlarged Ruler____

For each drawing do you have
headings and directions? Yes____ No____ Some ____
angle accuracy check? Yes____ No____ Some ____
ratio check? Yes____ No____ Some ____

CHECK

▪ IN THE INTRODUCTION DID YOU:
write as if the audience were the company president or______ ____
state the purpose of the report ____
describe the ruler with the extra space length between 0 and 1 ____
describe the ruler that is enlarged by some percent ____

TELLING SOMEONE WHERE TO GO 111

© 1994 THE REGENTS OF THE UNIVERSITY OF CALIFORNIA
LAWRENCE HALL OF SCIENCE, EQUALS INVESTIGATIONS: TELLING SOMEONE WHERE TO GO

Most teachers have students make the faulty instruments and use the instruments for re-drawing at least one set of directions in class. Many students will start out by checking effects only on special-case paths such as squares or regular polygons. Encourage these students to experiment with irregular, non-symmetrical paths as well. Be sure all students understand that if they use **Ratio Checks** then they should use real rulers to measure lengths, not the faulty instruments.

The main idea of an investigation is to explore some aspect of a situation in depth. Instead of just doing a bit on each instrument, you may want to encourage students to follow whatever path intrigues them. Someone may want to explore many cases of the effects of one particular instrument on trapezoidal paths, or the effects on navigation paths.

You may want each student to do a self-evaluation of their project before handing it in. The *Individual Project Self-Evaluation* (p. 111) may be given to each student and used as a cover sheet when the investigation is handed in.

✱ The Long Ruler has an effect similar to adding some amount to all lengths. The Enlarged Ruler has the same effect as multiplying all lengths by a number such as 1.4 and results in similar shapes. However, these conclusions are by no means all that can be said. Each student may come up with other interesting generalizations and ideas for effects on specific types of path shapes.

Family and Outside Help

On the *Individual Investigation*, help from family members and others should be encouraged. However, not all students have outside resources available to them and may need teacher intervention to insure an equitable experience. Remind students that the headings are measured LOGO-style. People who have studied only classical Euclidean geometry may focus on the interior angles of the paths rather than on the the headings.

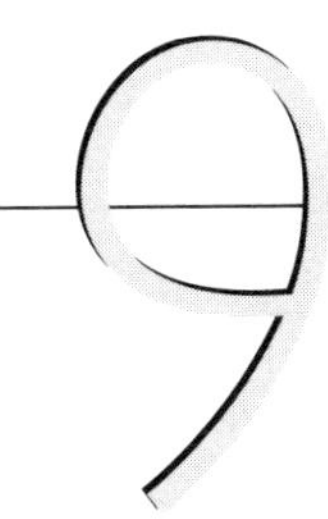

Sharing Individual Projects

End-of-unit Assessment

The best way for students to learn about quality is to recognize it in the work of their peers. The *Individual Projects* (p. 109) provide a golden opportunity for this kind of learning to take place. After *Individual Projects* have been handed in, set aside a day for students to share their projects with each other.

- MATERIALS: *Student worksheets:* End-of-unit Assessment *(p. 117),* Individual Investigation Seminar Questions *(p. 115).*
- TIME: *2 hours*

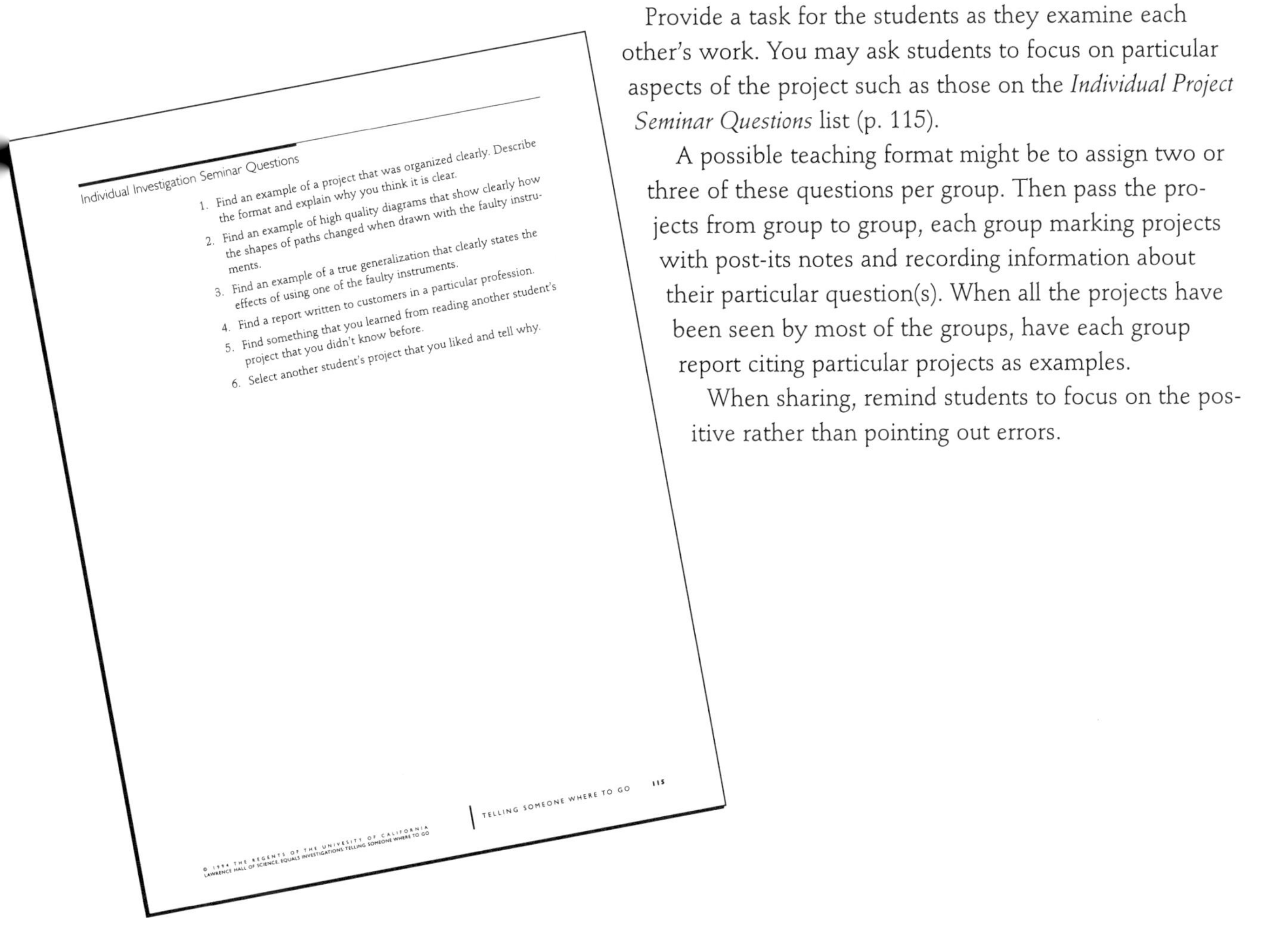

Individual Investigation Seminar Questions

1. Find an example of a project that was organized clearly. Describe the format and explain why you think it is clear.
2. Find an example of high quality diagrams that show clearly how the shapes of paths changed when drawn with the faulty instruments.
3. Find an example of a true generalization that clearly states the effects of using one of the faulty instruments.
4. Find a report written to customers in a particular profession.
5. Find something that you learned from reading another student's project that you didn't know before.
6. Select another student's project that you liked and tell why.

Provide a task for the students as they examine each other's work. You may ask students to focus on particular aspects of the project such as those on the *Individual Project Seminar Questions* list (p. 115).

A possible teaching format might be to assign two or three of these questions per group. Then pass the projects from group to group, each group marking projects with post-its notes and recording information about their particular question(s). When all the projects have been seen by most of the groups, have each group report citing particular projects as examples.

When sharing, remind students to focus on the positive rather than pointing out errors.

Telling Someone Where To Go End-Of-Unit Assessment

1. Write a letter to a seventh grader explaining how to use a protractor to measure and lay out angles.
2. Explain what a *Ratio Check* is and what it is used for.
3. Draw a path shaped like a bow tie. Measure and write the instructions so another person could draw it without seeing it.
4. Mark a starting point and accurately draw this path:
   1) 0°, go 6.6 cm
   2) Left 120°, go 8.4 cm
   3) Right 130°, go 6.0 cm
   Find the distance and heading that will return you to the starting point.
5. Here are the turns for a closed orienteering path with four legs:
   0°, Right 123°, Left 97°, Left 108°
   Walk this path back to its starting point. Find the amount of turn needed to return you to the exact same direction you started.
6. Describe what did you liked best/least about the *Telling Someone Where To Go* unit.
7. Describe what you would recommend for this unit regarding improvements or changes.
8. Write a good question that you think belongs on this assessment and answer it.

After students complete the *Individual Project,* you may also want to give them a final *End-of-Unit Assessment* (p. 117). During this assessment students should have open access to all their notes and work completed during the unit. Encourage them to cite specific examples from their work to support what they say. You may want to allow students to take the assessment home. Students may select two or three of the items to respond to, or you may assign particular questions and let them choose from others.

Answers:

#5 is Right 125° go 8.6 cm ; #6 is a bow-tie path so angles must sum to 0°. Therefore, the return angle is Right 82°.

BLACKLINE MASTERS

FOR TRANSPARENCIES AND STUDENT WORKSHEETS

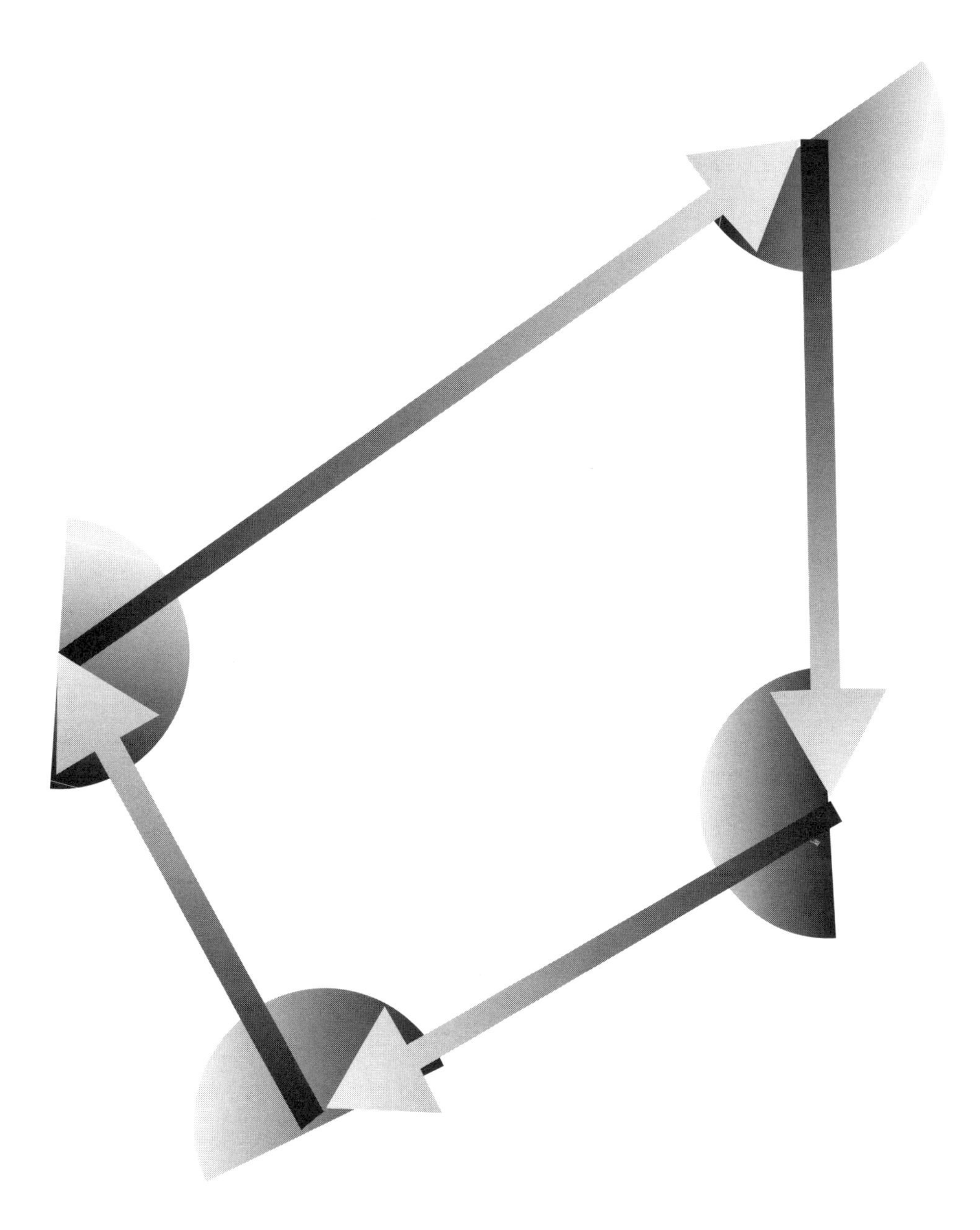

Dear Student and Family,

During the next several weeks we will be learning about the mathematics of navigation in a unit called *Telling Someone Where To Go*. To navigate from one place to another, distances and angles must be measured accurately, because the smallest errors may have disastrous results. Throughout this unit we will measure heading angles "LOGO-style," such as turn left 120° from the direction you are facing, rather than using magnetic compass headings, such as 30° to the west of north.

In addition to learning about measurement of angles and distances, we will practice many mathematical skills including the use of estimation, decimals, percents, fractions, ratios, spatial reasoning, and logic. We will design and conduct experiments, and draw conclusions from the results of those experiments.

Work will be easier if each student brings a centimeter ruler, calculator, and protractor to use in and outside of class. Having a sharp pencil and eraser will increase accuracy. The meter-cords and angle-ometers will be made in class with materials provided by the classroom teacher.

What are the expectations for students?

During this unit you will work in the same ways that mathematical work is done outside of school. In particular, you can expect to:

- Work in an assigned group and contribute to accomplishing the tasks assigned to your group.
- Produce several individual assignments and a project of your own near the end of the unit.
- Use your calculator skillfully. A calculator will be available at all times.
- Organize your own work instead of being told exactly how to present it.
- Demonstrate initiative, creativity, and mathematical knowledge.

For group work assigned to be done outside of the classroom, it may be necessary to contact other members of your group by telephone or meet with them outside of class. The individual project is your opportunity to show what you have learned during the unit. You may get help and advice from other people, but you are expected to do your own writing and thinking.

How can families help?

Give encouragement and support. At least every other day ask, "What are you working on in math class?" You will find out what we are doing and your child will have to do some thinking and reviewing. You may help your child with the mathematics if you wish, but please be sure he/she understands any special techniques you use.

____

your teacher

Estimado Estudiante y Familia,

Durante las próximas semanas vamos a estar aprendiendo sobre las matemáticas de navegación en una unidad que se llama, *Diciéndole A Alguien A Dónde Ir.* Para navegar de un lugar a otro, distancias y ángulos deben de ser medidos exactamente, porque los errores más pequeños pueden tener resultados desastrosos. Por toda esta unidad vamos a medir ángulos de orientación «LOGO-style». Por ejemplo, da una vuelta de 120º en la dirección en la cual estás mirando, en lugar de usar las orientaciones del compás magnético, como 30º para el oeste del Norte.

Además de aprender cómo medir los ángulos y las distancias, vamos a practicar destrezas de matemática, incluyendo el uso de la estimación, los decimales, los porcentajes, las fracciones, las raziones, el razonamiento espacial, y la lógica. Vamos a diseñar y conducir experimentos, y obtener conclusiones de los resultados de esos experimentos.

El trabajo será más fácil si cada estudiante trae una regla de centímetro, una calculadora y un transportador para usar dentro y fuera de la clase. El tener un lápiz puntiagudo y un borrador aumentará la precisión. Las cuerdas de un metro y los «angle-ometers» van a ser hechos en clase con materiales suplidos por la maestra de la clase.

¿Qué se espera de los estudiantes?

Durante esta unidad, trabajarás de maneras similares a las que se utilizan en ejecutar el trabajo matemático fuera de la escuela. En particular, puedes esperar lo siguiente:

- Trabajar en un grupo fijo y contribuir para completar las tareas asignadas a tu grupo.
- Producir muchas tareas individuales y un proyecto que sea tuyo cerca del final de la unidad.
- Usar tu calculadora hábilmente. Una calculadora será disponible a cada momento.
- Organizar tu propio trabajo en vez de que te digan exactamente cómo presentarlo.
- Demostrar iniciativa, creatividad, y un conocimiento de la matemática.

Para el trabajo de grupo asignado para hacerse fuera de la clase, quizás sea necesario ponerte en contacto con los miembros de tu grupo por teléfono o quizás tendrán que reunirse fuera de clase. El proyecto individual es tu oportunidad para demostrar lo que has aprendido en esta unidad. Puedes recibir ayuda y consejos de otras personas, pero se espera que hagas tu propio trabajo y razonamiento.

¿Cómo pueden ayudar las familias?

Dé alientamiento y apoyo. Por lo menos cada otro día pregúntele a su hijo/a, «¿en qué estás trabajando en la clase de matemática?» No solamente se dará cuenta de lo que estamos haciendo, pero también para poder contestar la pregunta, su hijo/a tendrá que realizar un poco de repaso y razonamiento individual. Si gusta, usted puede ayudarle a su hijo/a con las matemáticas, pero por favor, asegúrese de que el/ella entienda cualquier técnica especial que esté usando.

____

Su Maestro/a

Angle-ometer: A Mathematical Tool for Measuring Headings

Fold the paper to make a square so the angle-ometer scale just shows.

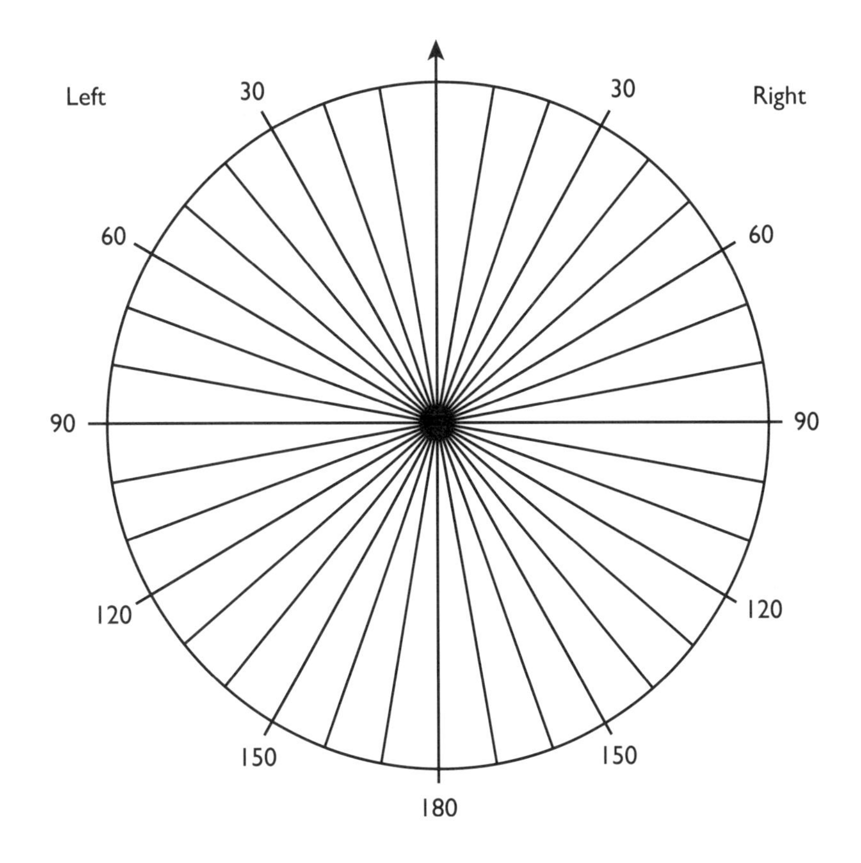

«Angle-ometer»: Una Herramienta de Matemática Para Medir Orientaciones

Dobla el papel, haciendo un cuadro, de modo que la escala del «angle-ometer» sea lo único que se vea.

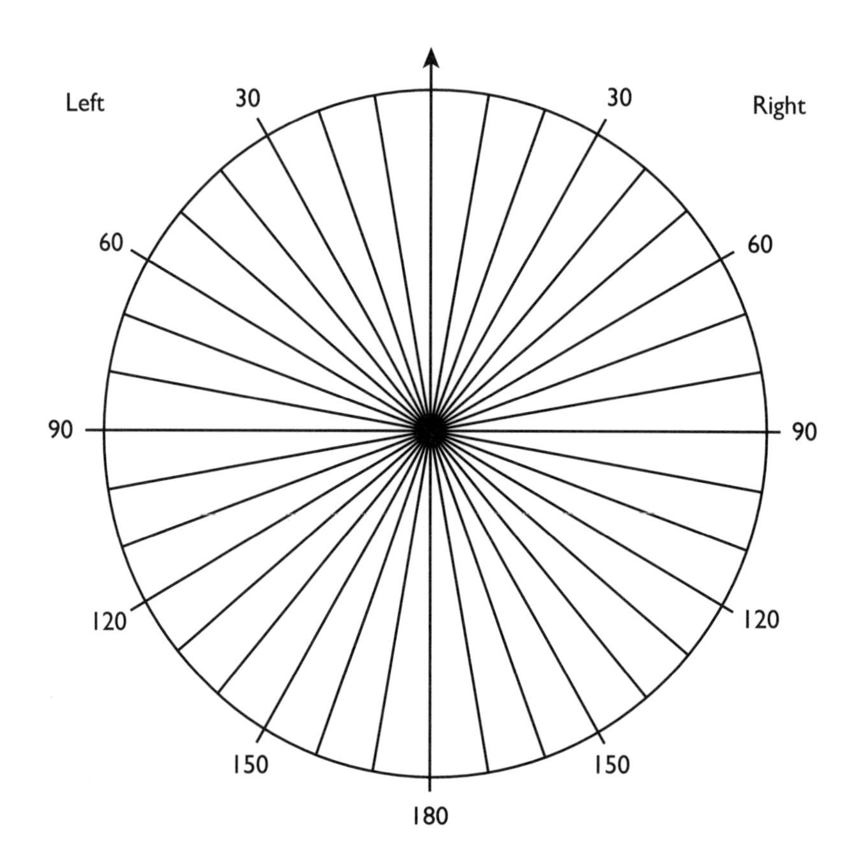

Names ______________ ______________

Date__________ Period ________ (One sheet per pair)

Walking Paths With the Angle-ometer #1

Follow each set of instructions. As you walk, make a sketch of each path in the space provided. Remember, the direction you are facing before each turn will always be considered as 0°.

1)
a. turn Right 90° go 3 paces
b. turn Right 90° go 3 paces
c. turn Right 90° go 6 paces
d. turn Right 90° go 7 paces
e. turn Right 90° go 6 paces

4)
a. turn 0° go 7 paces
b. turn Left 90° go 3 paces
c. turn Left 90° go 3 paces
d. turn Left 90° go 3 paces

2)
a. turn 0° go 4 paces
b. turn Left 90° go 4 paces
c. turn Left 90° go 4 paces
d. turn Left 90° go 4 paces

5)
a. turn Left 60° go 5 paces
b. turn Right 120° go 5 paces
c. turn Left 60° go 3 paces
d. turn Left 90° go 4 paces
e. turn Left 90° go 9 paces

3)
a. turn Left 90° go 4 paces
b. turn Right 120° go 5 paces
c. turn Right 120° go 7 paces

6)
a. turn Right 90° go 3 paces
b. turn Left 90° go 3 paces
c. turn Left 90° go 3 paces
d. turn Right 90° go 3 paces
e. turn Right 90° go 3 paces

Nombres ____________________ ______________________________

Fecha __________ Período (Una hoja para cada dos personas)_______

Senderos de Caminar con el «Angle-Ometer» #1

Sigue el par de instrucciones. Al caminar haz un esquema de cada sendero en el espacio dado. Acuérdate de que la dirección en que estás mirando, antes de dar cada vuelta, siempre será considerada como 0°.

1)
a. da vuelta a la derecha 90°, camina 3 pasos
b. da vuelta a la derecha 90°, camina 3 pasos
c. da vuelta a la derecha 90°, camina 6 pasos
d. da vuelta a la derecha 90°, camina 7 pasos
e. da vuelta a la derecha 90°, camina 6 pasos

2)
a. da vuelta 0° camina 4 pasos
b. da vuelta a la izquierda 90°, camina 4 pasos
c. da vuelta a la izquierda 90°, camina 4 pasos
d. da vuelta a la izquierda 90°, camina 4 pasos

3)
a. da vuelta a la izquierda 90°, camina 4 pasos
b. da vuelta a la derecha 120°, camina 5 pasos
c. da vuelta a la derecha 120°, camina 7 pasos

4)
a. da vuelta 0°, camina 7 pasos
b. da vuelta a la izquierda 90°, camina 3 pasos
c. da vuelta a la izquierda 90°, camina 3 pasos
d. da vuelta a la izquierda 90°, camina 3 pasos

5)
a. da vuelta a la izquierda 60°, camina 5 pasos
b. da vuelta a la derecha 120°, camina 5 pasos
c. da vuelta a la izquierda 60°, camina 3 pasos
d. da vuelta a la izquierda 90°, camina 4 pasos
e. da vuelta a la izquierda 90°, camina 9 pasos

6)
a. da vuelta a la derecha 90°, camina 3 pasos
b. da vuelta a la izquierda 90°, camina 3 pasos
c. da vuelta a la izquierda 90°, camina 3 pasos
d. da vuelta a la derecha 90°, camina 3 pasos
e. da vuelta a la derecha 90°, camina 3 pasos

Names ______________________ ____________________________

Date__________ Period ________ (One sheet per pair)

Walking Paths With the Angle-ometer #2

Follow each set of instructions. As you walk, make a sketch of each path in the space beside the instructions. Remember, the direction you are facing before each turn will always be considered as 0°.

1)
a. turn Right 60° go 10 paces
b. turn Right 120° go 5 paces
c. turn Right 120° go 10 paces
d. turn Left 120° go 5 paces

2)
a. turn Left 60° go 10 paces
b. turn Left 120° go 5 paces
c. turn Left 120° go 10 paces
d. turn Right 120° go 5 paces

3)
a. turn Right 45° go 10 paces
b. turn Right 45° go 7 paces
c. turn Right 90° go 7 paces
d. turn Right 45° go 10 paces
e. turn Right 90° go 10 paces

4)
a. turn 0° go 10 paces
b. turn Left 144° go 10 paces
c. turn Left 144° go 10 paces
d. turn Left 144° go 10 paces
e. turn Left 144° go 10 paces

5)
a. turn Right 45° go 12 paces
b. turn Left 90° go 6 paces
c. turn Left 90° go 6 paces
d. turn Left 90° go 12 paces
e. turn Right 135° go 7 paces

6)
a. turn 0° go 3 paces
b. turn Right 90° go 6 paces
c. turn Left 135° go 8 paces
d. turn Right 135° go 2 paces
e. turn Left 135° go 3 paces
f. turn Left 90° go 3 paces
g. turn Left 135° go 2 paces
h. turn Right 135° go 8 paces
i. turn Left 135° go 6 paces
j. turn Right 90° go 3 paces

Nombres ____________________ ______________________________

Fecha __________ Período (Una hoja para cada dos personas)_______

Senderos de Caminar con el «Angle-Ometer» #1

Sigue el par de instrucciones. Al caminar haz un esquema de cada sendero en el espacio dado. Acuérdate de que la dirección en que estás mirando, antes de dar cada vuelta, siempre será considerada como 0°.

1)
a. da vuelta a la derecha 60°, camina 10 pasos
b. da vuelta a la derecha 120°, camina 5 pasos
c. da vuelta a la derecha 120°, camina 10 pasos
d. da vuelta a la izquierda 120°, camina 5 pasos

2)
a. da vuelta a la izquierda 60°, camina 10 pasos
b. da vuelta a la izquierda 120°, camina 5 pasos
c. da vuelta a la izquierda 120°, camina 10 pasos
d. da vuelta a la derecha 120°, camina 5 pasos

3)
a. da vuelta a la derecha 45°, camina 10 pasos
b. da vuelta a la derecha 45°, camina 7 pasos
c. da vuelta a la derecha 90°, camina 7 pasos
d. da vuelta a la derecha 45°, camina 10 pasos
e. da vuelta a la derecha 90°, camina 10 pasos

4)
a. da vuelta 0°, camina 10 pasos
b. da vuelta a la izquierda 144°, camina 10 pasos
c. da vuelta a la izquierda 144°, camina 10 pasos
d. da vuelta a la izquierda 144°, camina 10 pasos
e. da vuelta a la izquierda 144°, camina 10 pasos

5)
a. da vuelta a la derecha 45°, camina 12 pasos
b. da vuelta a la izquicrda 90°, camina 6 pasos
c. da vuelta a la izquierda 90°, camina 6 pasos
d. da vuelta a la izquierda 90°, camina 12 pasos
e. da vuelta a la derecha 135°, camina 7 pasos

6)
a. da vuelta 0°, camina 3 pasos
b. da vuelta a la derecha 90°, camina 6 pasos
c. da vuelta a la izquierda 135°, camina 8 pasos
d. da vuelta a la derecha 135°, camina 2 pasos
e. da vuelta a la izquierda 135°, camina 3 pasos
f. da vuelta a la izquierda 90°, camina 3 pasos
g. da vuelta a la izquierda 135°, camina 2 pasos
h. da vuelta a la derecha 135°, camina 8 pasos
i. da vuelta a la izquierda 135°, camina 6 pasos
j. da vuelta a la derecha 90°, camina 3 pasos

Names ______________________ ____________________________

Date__________ Period _______ (One sheet per pair)

Walking Paths With the Angle-ometer Homework #2

For these problems, the direction you are facing before each turn will always be considered as 0°. This is the LOGO way of giving headings.

1. Sketch the path resulting from this set of instructions.

   Hint: Draw an eye in after you are done.

   a. turn Right 45° go 6 paces
   b. turn Left 120° go 12 paces
   c. turn Right 150° go 12 paces
   d. turn Left 60° go 10 paces
   e. turn Right 80° go 6 paces
   f. turn Right 140° go 4 paces
   g. turn Left 70° go 6 paces
   h. turn Left 80° go 12 paces
   i. turn Right 150° go 14 paces
   j. turn Right 90° go 8 paces

2. Write instructions for walking a path with this shape using paces and an angle-ometer.

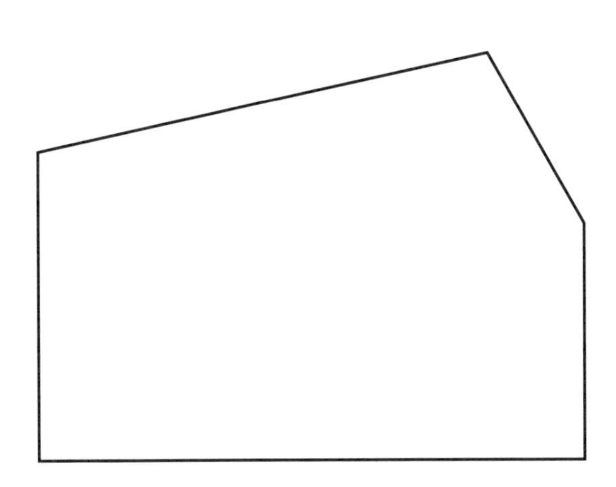

3. Suppose a set of instructions makes a rectangular-shaped path. What can you say that must be true about this set of instructions?

4. Sometimes a set of instructions creates a path which leads you back to your starting point. This kind of path is called a CLOSED PATH. On the back of the paper, sketch a closed path that has five turns. Then, write the instructions so another person could walk the path.

Nombres ____________________ ____________________________

Fecha __________ Período (Una hoja para cada dos personas)_______

Senderos de Caminar Con el «Angle-Ometer» Tarea #2

Para estos problemas, la dirección que estás mirando, antes de dar cada vuelta, siempre será considerada como 0°. Este es el logotipo para dar las orientaciones.

1. Haz un esquema del sendero que resultará de esta serie de instrucciones. Sugerencia: Dibuja un ojo después de que hayas terminado.

   a. da vuelta a la derecha 45°, camina 6 pasos
   b. da vuelta a la izquierda 120°, camina 12 pasos
   c. da vuelta a la derecha 150°, camina 12 pasos
   d. da vuelta a la izquierda 60°, camina 10 pasos
   e. da vuelta a la derecha 80°, camina 6 pasos
   f. da vuelta a la derecha 140°, camina 4 pasos
   g. da vuelta a la izquierda 70°, camina 6 pasos
   h. da vuelta a la izquierda 80°, camina 12 pasos
   i. da vuelta a la derecha 150°, camina 14 pasos
   j. da vuelta a la derecha 90°, camina 8 pasos

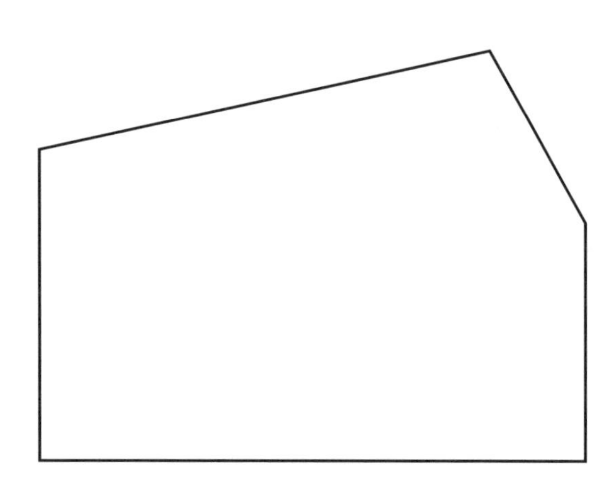

2. Escribe las instrucciones para caminar el sendero con esta figura, usando pasos y un «angle-ometer.»

3. Supón que una serie de instrucciones forme una figura rectangular de senderos. ¿Qué puedes decir acerca de estas instrucciones que sea verdad?

4. En veces una serie de instrucciones crean un sendero que te regresará al punto de partida. Este tipo de sendero se llama SENDERO CERRADO. Al otro lado de la hoja, dibuja un sendero cerrado que tenga cinco vueltas. Después, escribe las instrucciones para que otra persona pueda caminar el sendero.

Getting Around: Orienteering Paths (Outside Version)

- Mark your starting point with chalk, tape, or penny.
- Use your anglo-ometer and meter-cord to lay out the first 3 legs according to the distances and headings given.
- Find the return distance and heading that completes the closed quadrilateral path.
- Measure each distance to the nearest tenth of a meter and each heading to the nearest degree.

Path Q

Mark a starting point.
1) 0° go 4 m.
2) Right 60° go 3.2 m
3) Right 130° go 3.8 m
What distance and heading returns you to the starting point?

Path R

Mark a starting point.
1) 0° go 2.1 m
2) Left 50° go 2.9 m
3) Right 130° go 3.3 m
What distance and heading return you to the starting point?

Path S

Mark a starting point.
1) 0° go 1.6 m
2) Left 70° go 2.6 m
3) Right 110° go 3 m
What distance and heading return you to the starting point?

Path T

Mark a starting point.
1) 0° go 2.7 m
2) Left 110° go 4.1 m
3) Left 120° go 1.7 m
What distance and heading return you to the starting point?

Path V

Mark a starting point.
1) 0° go 3.3 m
2) Left 120° go 4.2 m
3) Right 130° go 3 m
What distance and heading return you to the starting point?

Path W

Mark a starting point.
1) 0° go 2.1 m
2) Left 40° go 3.9 m
3) Left 140° go 3.3 m
What distance and heading return you to the starting point?

Path Y

Mark a starting point.
1) 0° go 2 m
2) Right 70° go 3.4 m
3) Left 140° go 1.4 m
What distance and heading return you to the starting point?

Path Z

Mark a starting point.
1) 0° go 3.5 m
2) Right 140° go 3 m
3) Left 130° go 2.4 m
What distance and heading return you to the starting point?

- Señala tu punto de partida con una tiza, una cinta adhesiva, o un centavo.
- Usa tu «angle-ometer» y un metro de cuerda para poner las 3 piernas, según las distancias y las orientaciones dadas.
- Encuentra la distancia de regreso y la orientación que complete el sendero cuadrilátero cerrado.
- Mide cada distancia al más cercano décimo de un metro y cada orientación al más cercano grado.

Sendero Curso Q

Marca un punto de partida.
1) Da vuelta 0°, camina 4 m
2) Da vuelta 60° a la derecha, camina 3.2 m
3) Da vuelta 130° a la derecha, camina 3.8 m
¿Qué distancia y orientación te regresará al punto de partida?

Sendero Curso R

Marca un punto de partida.
1) Da vuelta 0°, camina 2.1 m
2) Da vuelta 50° a la izquierda, camina 2.9 m
3) Da vuelta 130° a la derecha, camina 3.3 m
¿Qué distancia y orientación te regresará al punto de partida?

Sendero Curso S

Marca un punto de partida.
1) Da vuelta 0°, camina 1.6 m
2) Da vuelta 70° a la izquierda, camina 2.6 m
3) Da vuelta 110° a la derecha, camina 3 m
¿Qué distancia y orientación te regresará al punto de partida?

Sendero Curso T

Marca un punto de partida.
1) Da vuelta 0°, camina 2.7 m
2) Da vuelta 110° a la izquierda, camina 4.1 m
3) Da vuelta 120° a la izquierda, camina 1.7 m
¿Qué distancia y orientación te regresará al punto de partida?

Sendero Curso V

Marca un punto de partida.
1) Da vuelta 0°, camina 3.3 m
2) Da vuelta 120° a la izquierda, camina 4.2 m
3) Da vuelta 130° a la derecha, camina 3 m
¿Qué distancia y orientación te regresará al punto de partida?

Sendero Curso W

Marca un punto de partida.
1) Da vuelta 0°, camina 2.1 m
2) Da vuelta 40° a la izquierda, camina 3.9 m
3) Da vuelta 140° a la izquierda, camina 3.3 m
¿Qué distancia y orientación te regresará al punto de partida?

Sendero Curso Y

Marca un punto de partida.
1) Da vuelta 0°, camina 2 m
2) Da vuelta 70° a la derecha, camina 3.4 m
3) Da vuelta 140° a la izquierda, camina 1.4 m
¿Qué distancia y orientación te regresará al punto de partida?

Sendero Curso Z

Marca un punto de partida.
1) Da vuelta 0°, camina 3.5 m
2) Da vuelta 140° a la derecha, camina 3 m
3) Da vuelta 130° a la izquierda, camina 2.4 m
¿Qué distancia y orientación te regresará al punto de partida?

- Mark your starting point with chalk, tape, or penny.
- Use your anglo-ometer and meter-cord to lay out the first 3 legs according to the distances and headings given.
- Find the return distance and heading that completes the closed quadrilateral path.
- Measure each distance to the nearest tenth of a meter and each heading to the nearest degree.

Path Q

Mark a starting point.
1) 0°, go 40 cm
2) Right 60°, go 32 cm
3) Right 130°, go 38 cm
What distance and heading return you to the starting point?

Path R

Mark a starting point.
1) 0°, go 21 cm
2) Left 50°, go 29 cm
3) Right 130°, go 33 cm
What distance and heading return you to the starting point?

Path S

Mark a starting point.
1) 0°, go 16 cm
2) Left 70°, go 26 cm
3) Right 110°, go 30 cm
What distance and heading return you to the starting point?

Path T

Mark a starting point.
1) 0°, go 27 cm
2) Left 110°, go 41 cm
3) Left 120°, go 17 cm
What distance and heading return you to the starting point?

Path V

Mark a starting point.
1) 0°, go 33 cm
2) Left 120°, go 42 cm
3) Right 130°, go 30 cm
What distance and heading return you to the starting point?

Path W

Mark a starting point.
1) 0°, go 21 cm
2) Left 40°, go 39 cm
3) Left 140°, go 33 cm
What distance and heading return you to the starting point?

Path Y

Mark a starting point.
1) 0°, go 20 cm
2) Right 70°, go 34 cm
3) Left 140°, go 14 cm
What distance and heading return you to the starting point?

Path Z

Mark a starting point.
1) 0°, go 35 cm
2) Right 140°, go 30 cm
3) Left 130°, go 24 cm
What distance and heading return you to the starting point?

- Señala tu punto de partida con una tiza, una cinta adhesiva, o un centavo.
- Usa tu «angle-ometer» y un metro de cuerda para poner las 3 piernas, según las distancias y las orientaciones dadas.
- Encuentra la distancia de regreso y la orientación que complete el sendero cuadrilátero cerrado.
- Mide cada distancia al más cercano décimo de un metro y cada orientación al más cercano grado.

Sendero Curso Q

Marca un punto de partida.
1) Da vuelta 0°, camina 40 cm
2) Da vuelta 60° a la derecha, camina 32 cm
3) Da vuelta 130° a la derecha, camina 38 cm
¿Qué distancia y orientación te regresará al punto de partida?

Sendero Curso R

Marca un punto de partida.
1) Da vuelta 0°, camina 21 cm
2) Da vuelta 50° a la izquierda, camina 29 cm
3) Da vuelta 130° a la derecha, camina 33 cm
¿Qué distancia y orientación te regresará al punto de partida?

Sendero Curso S

Marca un punto de partida.
1) Da vuelta 0°, camina 16 cm
2) Da vuelta 70° a la izquierda, camina 26 cm
3) Da vuelta 110° a la derecha, camina 30 cm
¿Qué distancia y orientación te regresará al punto de partida?

Sendero Curso T

Marca un punto de partida.
1) Da vuelta 0°, camina 27 cm
2) Da vuelta 110° a la izquierda, camina 41 cm
3) Da vuelta 120° a la izquierda, camina 17 cm
¿Qué distancia y orientación te regresará al punto de partida?

Sendero Curso V

Marca un punto de partida.
1) Da vuelta 0°, camina 33 cm
2) Da vuelta 120° a la izquierda, camina 42 cm
3) Da vuelta 130° a la derecha, camina 30 cm
¿Qué distancia y orientación te regresará al punto de partida?

Sendero Curso W

Marca un punto de partida.
1) Da vuelta 0°, camina 21 cm
2) Da vuelta 40° a la izquierda, camina 39 cm
3) Da vuelta 140° a la izquierda, camina 33 cm
¿Qué distancia y orientación te regresará al punto de partida?

Sendero Curso Y

Marca un punto de partida.
1) Da vuelta 0°, camina 20cm
2) Da vuelta 70° a la derecha, camina 34 cm
3) Da vuelta 140° a la izquierda, camina 14 cm
¿Qué distancia y orientación te regresará al punto de partida?

Sendero Curso Z

Marca un punto de partida.
1) Da vuelta 0°, camina 35 cm
2) Da vuelta 140° a la derecha, camina 30 cm
3) Da vuelta 130° a la izquierda, camina 24 cm
¿Qué distancia y orientación te regresará al punto de partida?

Names ______________________ ____________________________

Date__________ Period _______ (One sheet per pair)

Getting Around: Orienteering Worksheet

- Copy the course letter and instructions for your course into the spaces.
- Lay out your course and make a rough sketch of it in the space to the right beside the instructions below.
- Measure your return heading and distance and write it into the space.

Orienteering Path: Course ___

Mark a starting point.

Path's Shape

1) _______________________

2) _______________________

3) _______________________

What distance and heading will return you to the starting point?

____

- What strategies have you and your partner used to increase your measurement accuracy when using the anglo-ometer and meter-cord?

100 points is a perfect score.

1 point is deducted for each whole tenth of a meter error in distance and

10 points are deducted for each whole 10° of heading error.

Score ________

Nombres ____________ ____________

Fecha ________ Período ____ (Una hoja para cada dos personas)

Viajando: Orientando Hoja de Orientación

- Copea la letra del curso y las instrucciones para tu curso en los espacios.
- Coloca tu curso y haz un esquema de el en el espacio que está a la derecha, cerca de las instrucciones, las cuales están más abajo.
- Mide tu orientación de regreso y la distancia, y escríbelo en el espacio.

Orientando Senderos: Curso___

Figura Del Sendero.

Señala el punto de partida.

1) ____________

2) ____________

3) ____________

¿Qué distancia y orientación te regresará al punto de partida?

____

- ¿Qué estrategias han usado, tú y tu compañero, para aumentar la exactitud de medidas, cuando usan su «angle-ometer» y el metro de cuerda?

100 puntos es una puntuación perfecta.
Un punto es quitado para cada error de un décimo entero para un metro en distancia y 10 puntos son quitados para errores de cada 10 grados enteros en la orientación.

Puntuación ________

The New York Times

NEW YORK, SATURDAY,MARCH 25, 1989

1 *Largest U.S. Tanker Spill Spews Oil Off Alaska Coast*

THE NEW YORK TIMES

THE ENVIRONMENT

TUESDAY, APRIL 4, 1989

Veterinarians and volunteers join to wash off the oil.

By Malcolm W. Browne

Special to the New York Times

Valdez, Alaska, April 3—Casualties by the hundreds are pouring into a makeshift hospital for oil-soaked animals here, where conditions have begun to resemble those in a battle-field aid situation.

The Valdez Bird and Animal Rescue Center was created on March 24, within hours after the tanker Exxon Valdez ran aground on a reef 14 miles south of here. Since then, three gashes in the tanker hull have poured about 10 million gallons of crude oil into Prince William Sound, killing or endangering great numbers of animals.

For more than a week after the accident, few animals injured by the oil spill were found or collected. But by last weekend the flood of victims began, and veterinarians were getting little sleep.

"This place is like a MASH unit at this point." Ms. Berkner said. "We have to work as fast as we can to stay ahead of the game."

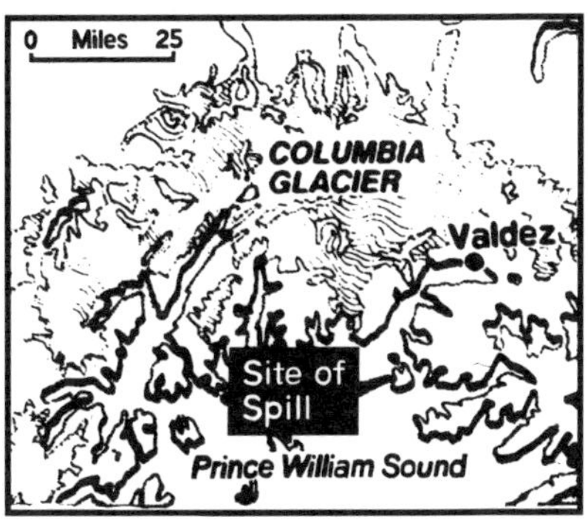

The New York Times/March 25, 1989

2 Exxon Vessel Hits Reef, Fouling Water That Is Rich in Marine Life

By Philip Shabecoff

A tanker filled to capacity with crude oil ran aground and ruptured yesterday 25 miles from the southern end of the Trans Alaska Pipeline, spewing her cargo into water rich in marine life.

By evening the ship, the Exxon Valdez, had sent more than 270,000 barrels of oil into Prince William Sound, making this the largest tanker spill in United States history.

3 *THE NEW YORK TIMES* NATIONAL THURSDAY, FEBRUARY 15, 1990

Mate on Tanker Faults Helmsman in Accident

Second Day on Stand

This was the second day of Mr. Cousins's testimony in Anchorage Superior Court, where the 43-year-old Captain Hazelwood is standing trial on one felony count of second-degree criminal mischief and misdemeanor charges of reckless endangerment, negligent discharge of oil and operating a vessel while intoxicated. The maximum penalty for conviction on all counts is seven years, three months in prison and fines totaling $61,000.

The cross-examination was conducted by Dick Madson, who asked the witness, "Mr. Cousins, isn't it correct that in your mind there's no doubt that if that 10-degree right rudder had been executed, the ship would have cleared Bligh Reef by a substantial margin?"

"That's my belief," Mr. Cousins said.

Mr. Cousins described the night of the accident as extremely dark and misty. He said that about an hour before the grounding on the ship's radar screen he spotted ice in the channel. It was too dark to actually see the ice from the deck. Mr. Cousins said, but he reported it to Captain Hazelwood, who decided to divert the tanker from normal shipping lanes.

Mr. Cousins and a helmsman. Robert Kagan, were at the wheel when the 987-foot tanker ran aground, spilling nearly 11 million gallons of crude oil in the nation's worst oil spill.

Grounding Interrupts Call

Mr. Cousins said that before he called he began to believe that Mr. Kagan was not properly following his orders to make a sharp change in the ship's course.

Mr. Cousins testified today that he had never worked with Mr. Kagan before and had heard rumors the seaman had problems with steering on another voyage.

The testimony came in the cross-examination by Captain Hazelwood's lawyer, who sought to show that all the procedures aboard the tanker were moving smoothly until the helmsman failed to execute a 10-degree right turn.

Mr. Cousins, who was told by Captain Hazelwood to take command of the tanker about 10 minutes before it went aground, suggested that Mr. Kagan caused the spill by not following orders to turn the wheel hard.

He said he was convinced that had the helmsman followed orders, the ship would have missed by several miles the rocky reef that she ultimately hit.

The New York Times

NUEVA YORK, SÁBADO 25 DE MARZO DE 1989

1 *El Derramiento del Buque Petrolero de Los Estados Unidos, Arroja Petróleo en la Costa de Alaska*

THE NEW YORK TIMES
EL AMBIENTE
martes 4 de abril de 1989

Veterinarios y voluntarios se unen para limpiar el petróleo.

Por Malcolm W. Browne

Valdez, Alaska, 3 de abril – Víctimas por los cienes están llegando en abundancia a los hospitales para animales empapados de petróleo aquí, en donde las condiciones empiezan a parecerse a esas en una estación de batalla de primeros auxilios.

El Valdez Bird y El Centro de Rescate de Animales se creó dentro de unas horas después que el tanque Exxon Valdez navegó encallado de un escollo a 14 millas sur de aquí. Desde entonces, tres cuchilladas en el hollejo del tanque vaciaron unos 10 millones de galones de petróleo crudo en Prince William Sound, matando o poniendo en peligro grandes números de animales.

Por más de una semana después del accidente, se encontraron y fueron colectados muy pocos animales heridos por el derramiento de petróleo. Pero, el fin de semana pasado, la inundación de víctimas empezó, y los veterinarios dormían muy poco.

«Este lugar es como una unidad de MASH,» dice la Sra. Barker. «Tenemos que trabajar lo más rápido posible para quedarnos adelantados del juego.»

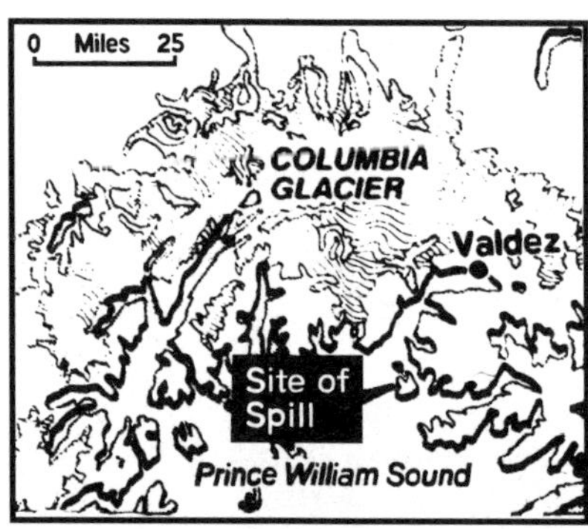

The New York Times/March 25, 1989

2 Tanque Exxon le Llega a un Escollo, Contaminando Agua Rica en Vida Marina

Por Philip Shabecoff

Un tanque lleno de petróleo crudo, navegó encallado de un escollo y se fracturó ayer 25 millas de la orilla al sur de la Trans Alaska Pipeline, arrojando su cargo en aguas ricas de vida marina.

Al anochecer, el barco, el Exxon Valdez, había vaciado más de 270,000 barriles de petróleo en Prince William Sound, haciendo este el derramiento de tanque más grande en la historia de los Estados Unidos.

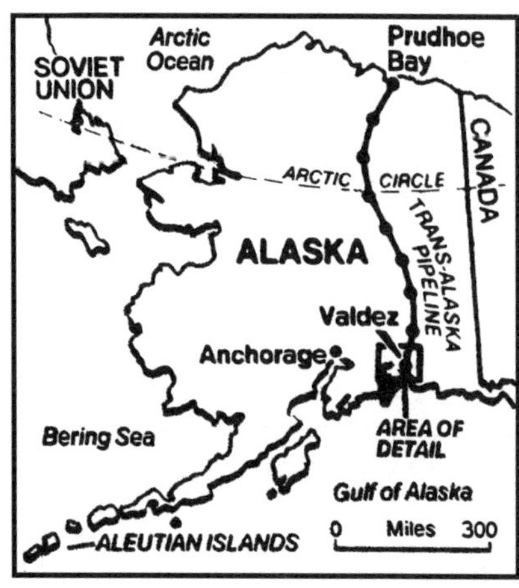

3 *THE NEW YORK TIMES* NATIONAL JUEVES 15 DE FEBRERO DE 1990

Un Compañero en el Tanque Culpa a un Encargado del Movimiento de Timón con el Accidente

Segundo día en el estrado

Este fue el segundo día del testimonio del Sr. Cousins en la Corte Superior de Anchorage, en donde el Capitán Hazelwood de 43 años de edad, está sujeto a juicio a cargo de una felonía de segundo grado de malicia criminal y cargos de celito menor por poner en peligro inprudentemente, descuidadosamente derramando petróleo, y operando un tanque bajo la influencia de alcohol. El castigo máximo por convicción en todos los cargos es de siete años, tres meses en la prisión y multas de $61,000 en total.

El interrogatorio riguroso fue conducido por Dick Madson, quien le preguntó al testigo de descargo, «Sr. Cousins, ¿No es correcto que en su mente, no hay duda que si el timón de 10 grados a la derecha se hubiera ejecutado, el barco no hubiera navegado encallado del Escollo Bligh por una margen substancial?»

«Eso es lo que creo,» dijo el Sr. Cousins.

El Sr. Cousins describió la noche del accidente como una noche extremamente oscura y nebulosa. El dice que una hora antes del encallado en la pantalla de radar del barco notó hielo en el canal. Estaba muy oscuro para poder ver actualmente el hielo de la bodega del barco, dijo el Sr. Cousins, pero se lo reportó al Capitán Hazelwood, quien decidió desviar el tanque de los senderos normales.

El Sr. Cousins y un hombre encargado del movimiento del timón del tanque, Robert Kagan, estaban en el timón cuando el tanque de 987 pies navegó encallado, derramando casi 11 millones de galones de petróleo crudo en el peor derramiento de petróleo de la nación.

El Encallo Interrumpe la Llamada

El Sr. Cousins dice que antes de llamar, él empezo a creer que el Sr. Kagan no estaba siguiendo sus órdenes apropiadamente para cambiar el curso riguroso del tanque.

El Sr. Cousins declaró hoy que nunca había trabajado con el Sr. Kagan antes y que había oido rumores que el marinero había tenido problemas conduciendo en otro viaje.

El testimonio vino en el interrogatorio riguroso por el licenciado del Capitán Hazelwood, quien quería demostrar que todos los procedimientos en el tanque se movían suavemente, hasta que el marinero falló en ejecutar la vuelta recta de 10 grados.

El Sr. Cousins, a quien el Capitán Hazelwood le había dicho que tomará poder del tanque unos diez minutos antes de encallarse, sugerió que el Sr. Kagan causó el derramiento al no seguir las órdenes de darle vuelta al timón fuerte.

Dice que estaba convencido que si el marinero hubiera seguido sus instrucciones, el tanque no le hubiera pegado por varias millas al escollo que le pegó.

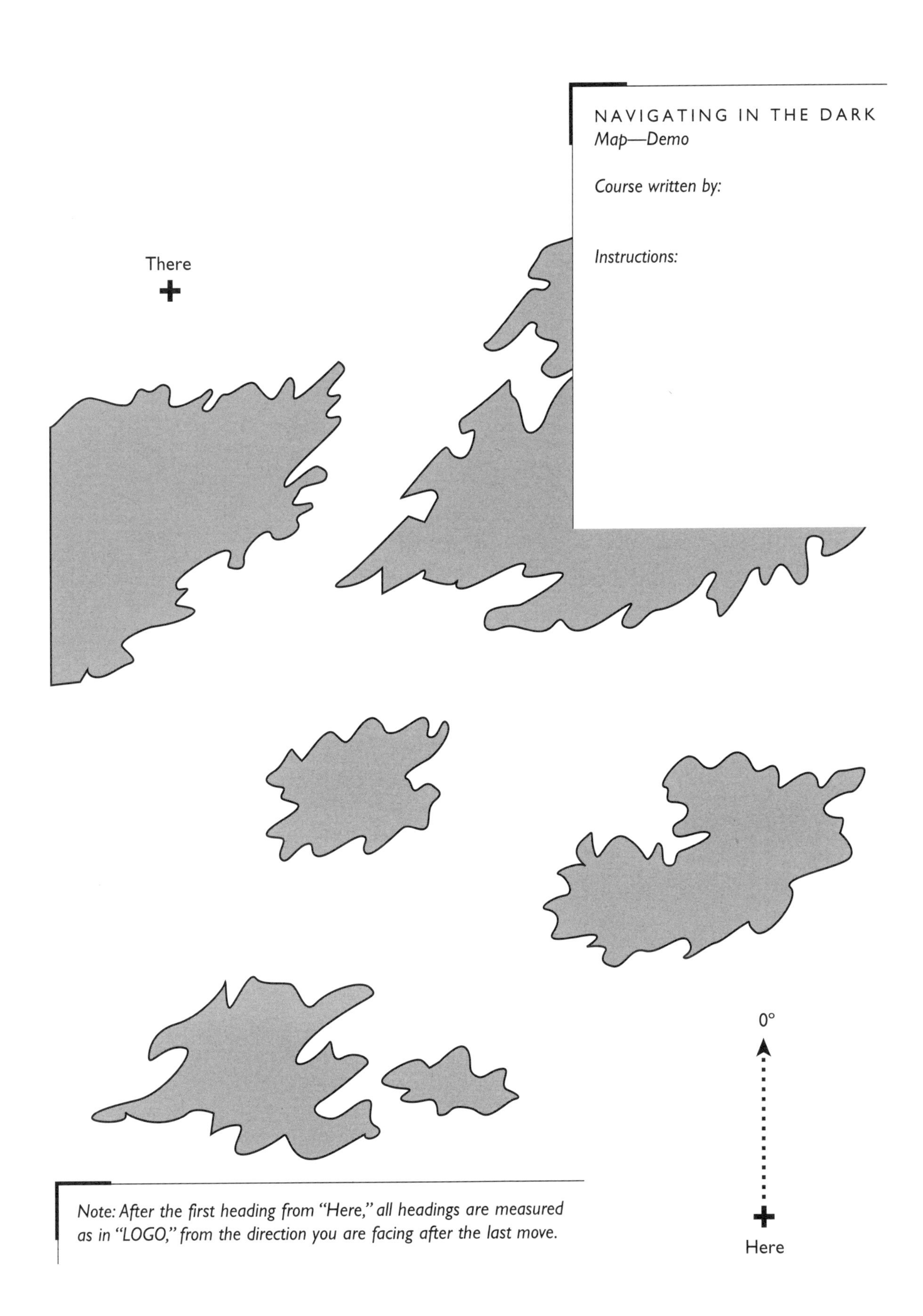

Note: After the first heading from "Here," all headings are measured as in "LOGO," from the direction you are facing after the last move.

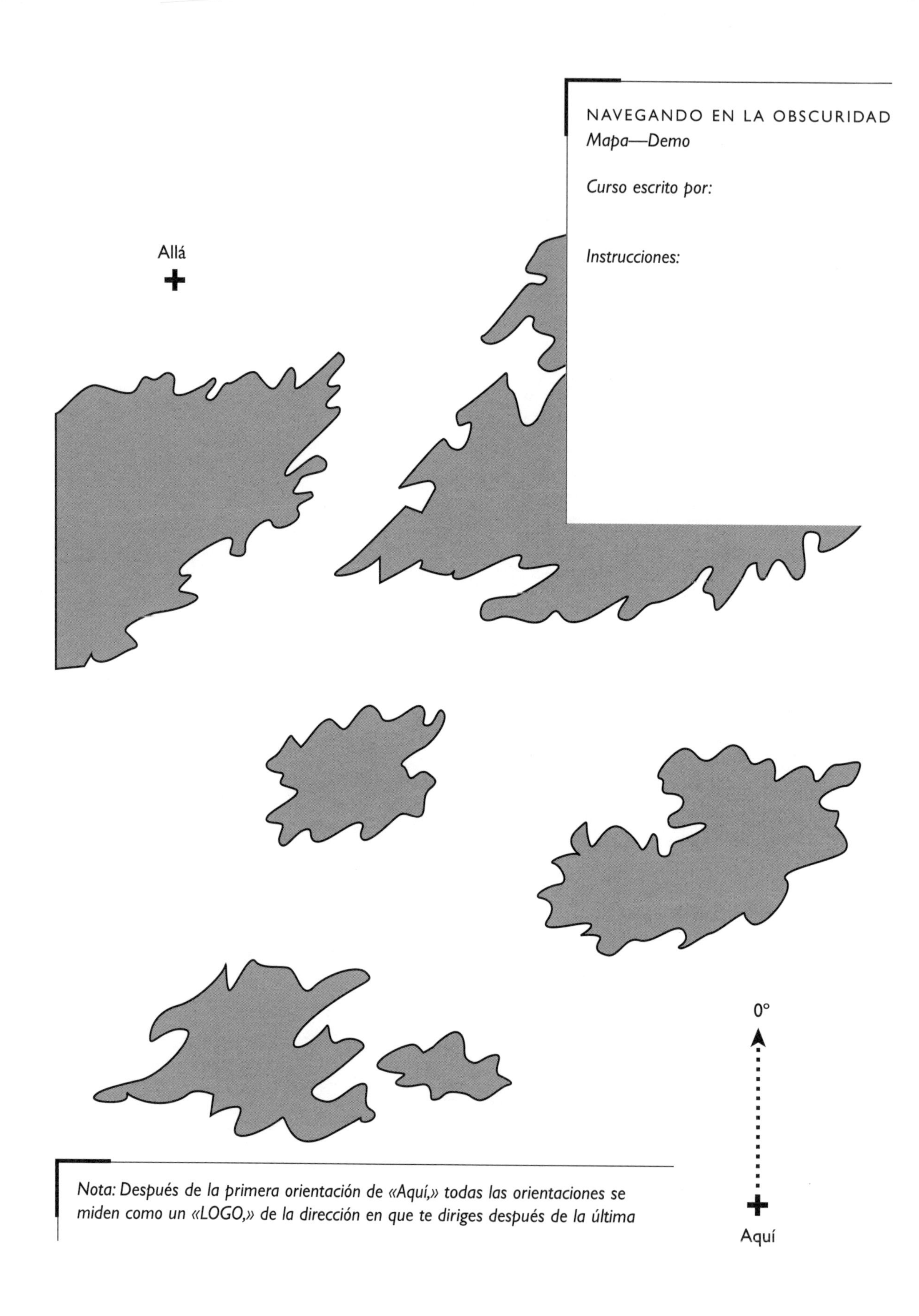
NAVEGANDO EN LA OBSCURIDAD
Mapa—Demo
Curso escrito por:
Instrucciones:
Allá
0°
Aquí
Nota: Después de la primera orientación de «Aquí,» todas las orientaciones se miden como un «LOGO,» de la dirección en que te diriges después de la última

NAVIGATING IN THE DARK
Map—

Course written by:

Course navigated by:

Instructions:

There
+

Note: After the first heading from "Here," all headings are measured as in "LOGO," from the direction you are facing after the last move.

NAVEGANDO EN LA OBSCURIDAD

Mapa—

Curso escrito por:

Curso navegado por:

Instrucciones:

Allá

+

Nota: Después de la primera orientación de «Aquí,» todas las orientaciones se miden como un «LOGO» de la dirección en que te diriges después de la última

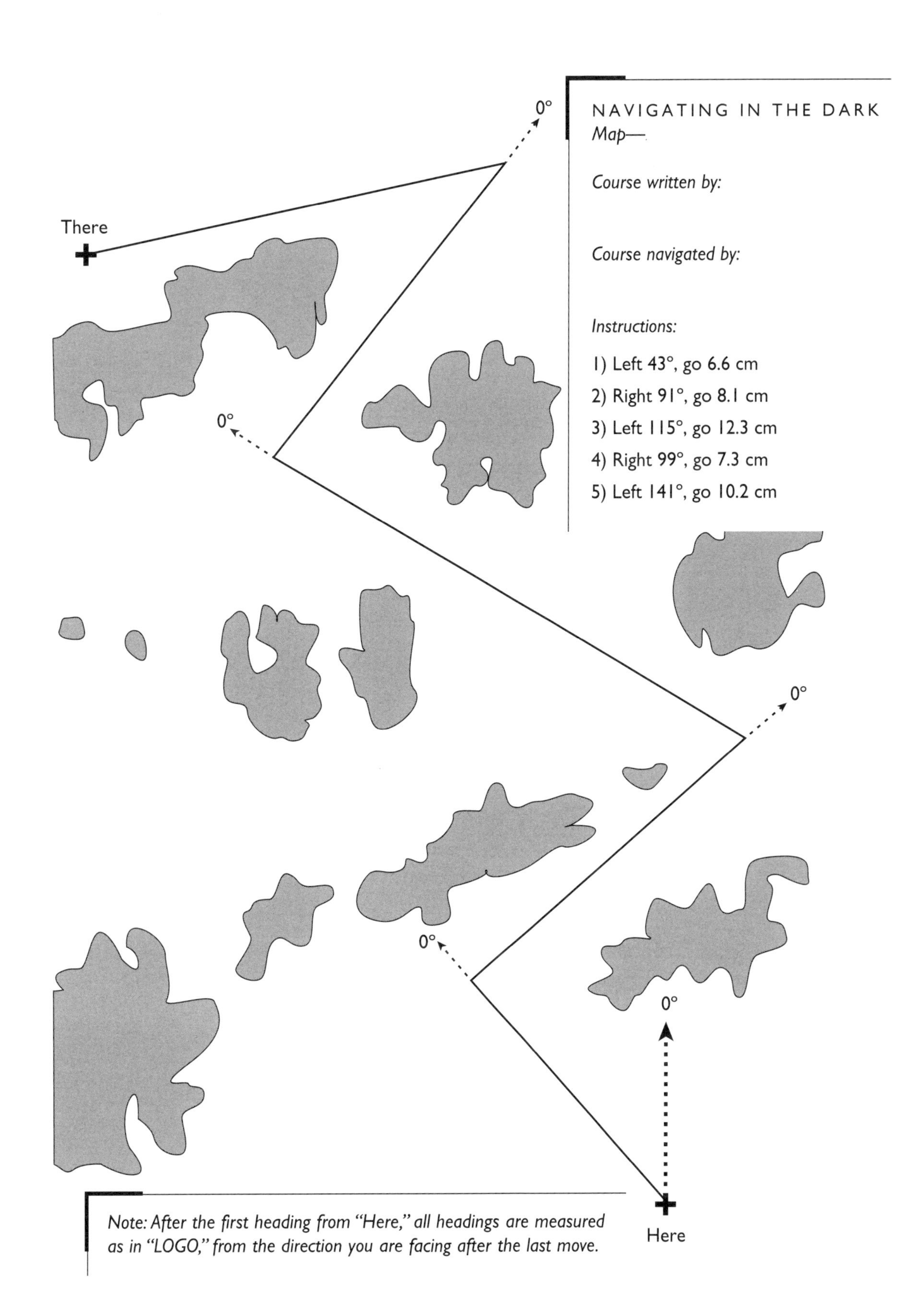

NAVIGATING IN THE DARK

Map—

Course written by:

Course navigated by:

Instructions:

1) Left 43°, go 6.6 cm
2) Right 91°, go 8.1 cm
3) Left 115°, go 12.3 cm
4) Right 99°, go 7.3 cm
5) Left 141°, go 10.2 cm

Note: After the first heading from "Here," all headings are measured as in "LOGO," from the direction you are facing after the last move.

NAVEGANDO EN LA OBSCURIDAD

Mapa—

Curso escrito por:

Curso navegado por:

Instrucciones:

1) Da vuelta 43° a la izquierda, camina 6.6 cm

2) Da vuelta 91° a la derecha, camina 8.1 cm

3) Da vuelta 115° a la izquierda, camina 12.3 cm

4) Da vuelta 99° a la derecha, camina 7.3 cm

5) Da vuelta 141° a la izquierda, camina 10.2 cm

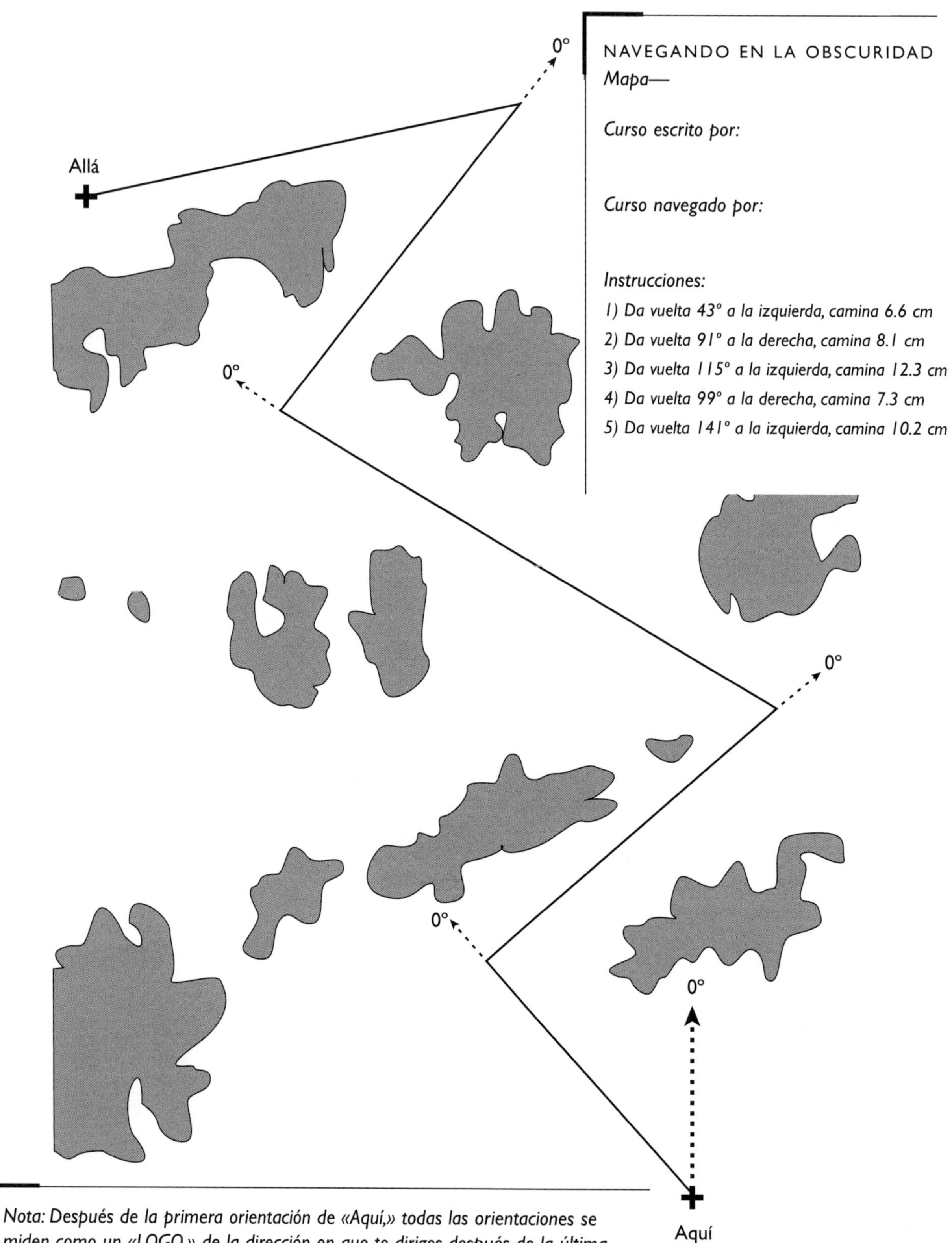

Nota: Después de la primera orientación de «Aquí,» todas las orientaciones se miden como un «LOGO,» de la dirección en que te diriges después de la última

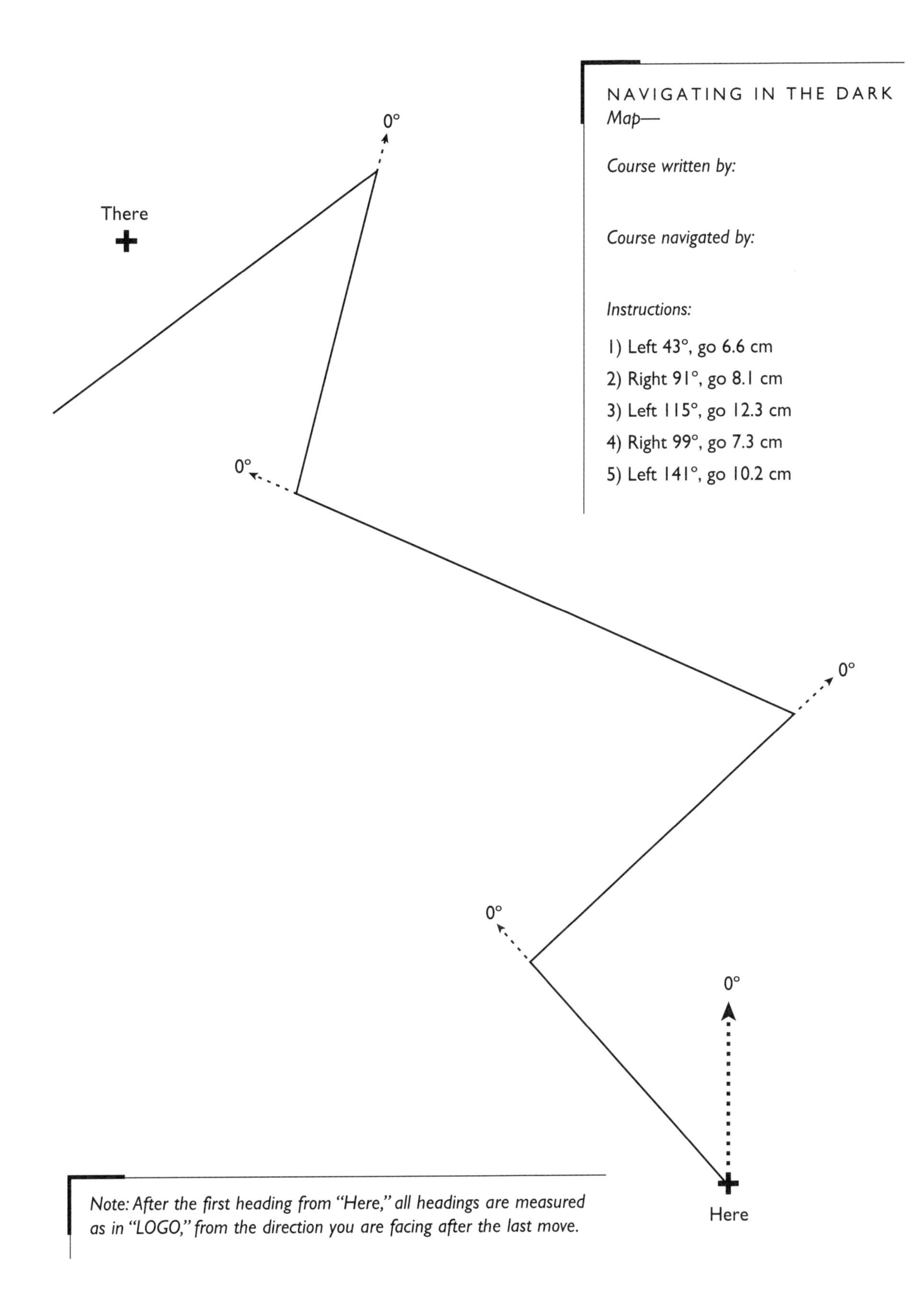

NAVIGATING IN THE DARK
Map—

Course written by:

Course navigated by:

Instructions:

1) Left 43°, go 6.6 cm
2) Right 91°, go 8.1 cm
3) Left 115°, go 12.3 cm
4) Right 99°, go 7.3 cm
5) Left 141°, go 10.2 cm

Note: After the first heading from "Here," all headings are measured as in "LOGO," from the direction you are facing after the last move.

NAVEGANDO EN LA OBSCURIDAD

Mapa—

Curso escrito por:

Curso navegado por:

Instrucciones:

1) Da vuelta 43° a la izquierda, camina 6.6 cm
2) Da vuelta 91° a la derecha, camina 8.1 cm
3) Da vuelta 115° a la izquierda, camina 12.3 cm
4) Da vuelta 99° a la derecha, camina 7.3 cm
5) Da vuelta 141° a la izquierda, camina 10.2 cm

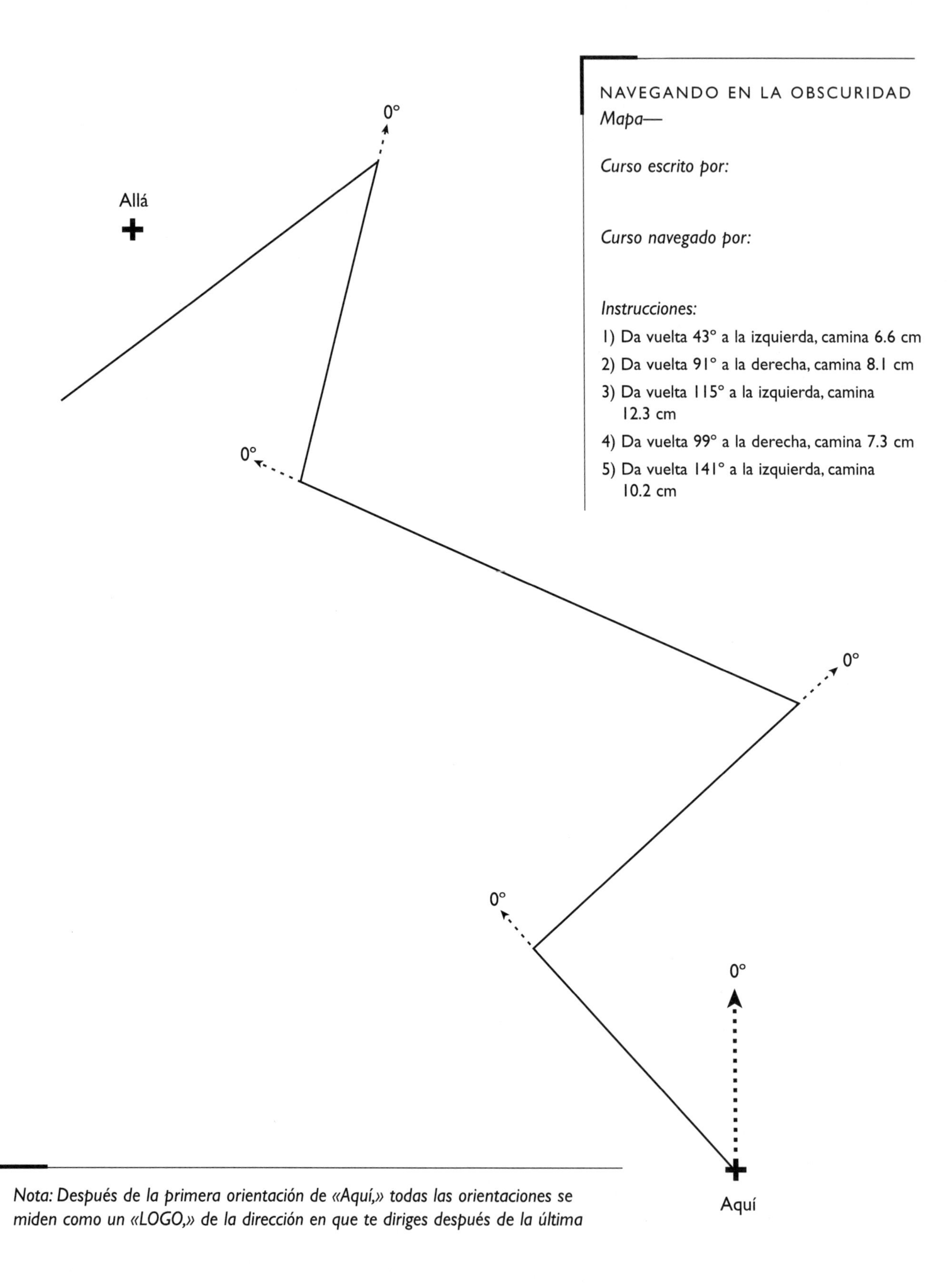

Nota: Después de la primera orientación de «Aquí,» todas las orientaciones se miden como un «LOGO,» de la dirección en que te diriges después de la última

NAVIGATING IN THE DARK

Map—1

Course written by:

Instructions:

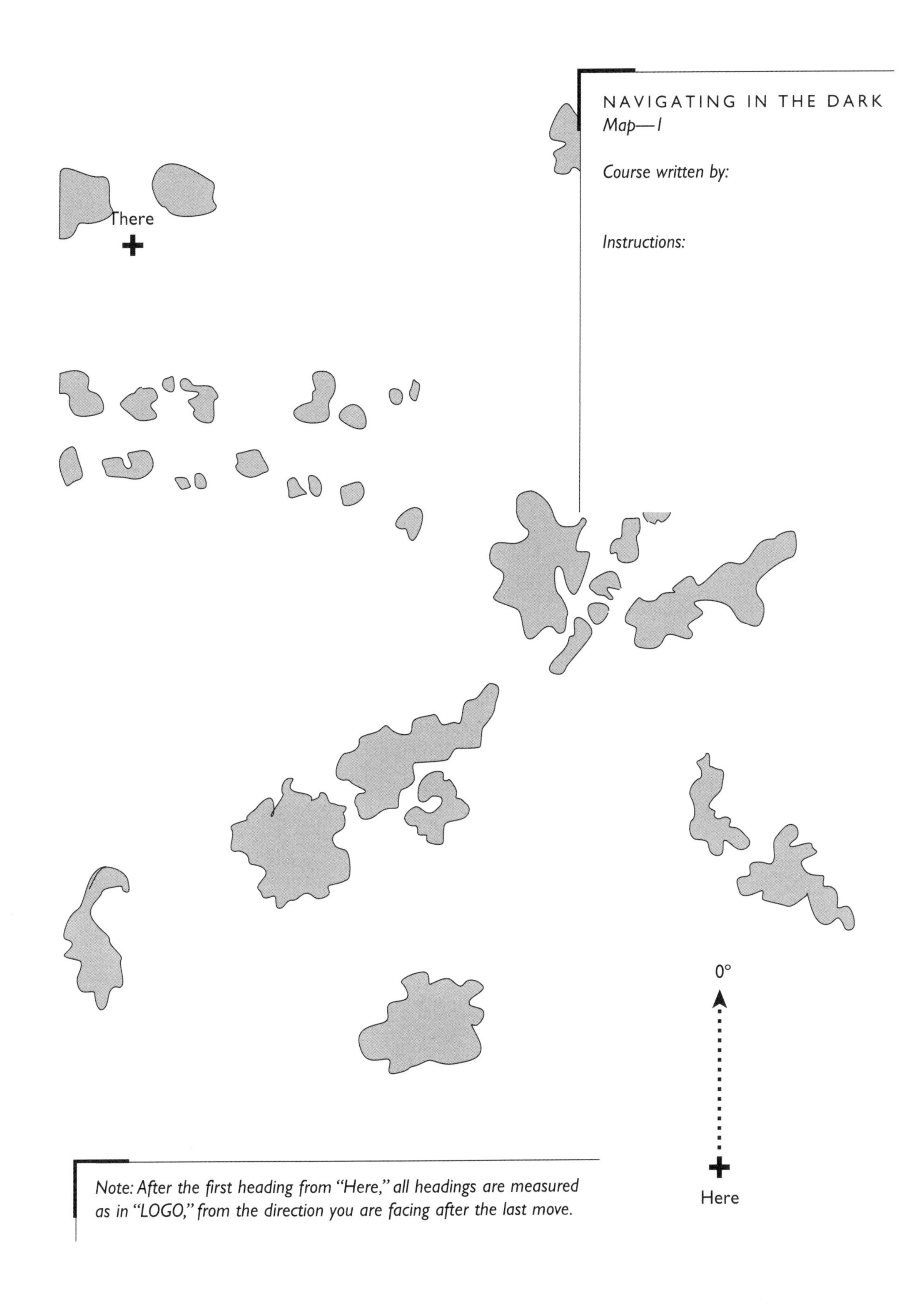

Note: After the first heading from "Here," all headings are measured as in "LOGO," from the direction you are facing after the last move.

Nota: Después de la primera orientación de «Aquí,» todas las orientaciones se miden como un «LOGO,» de la dirección en que te diriges después de la última movida.

NAVIGATING IN THE DARK

Map— 2

Course written by:

Instructions:

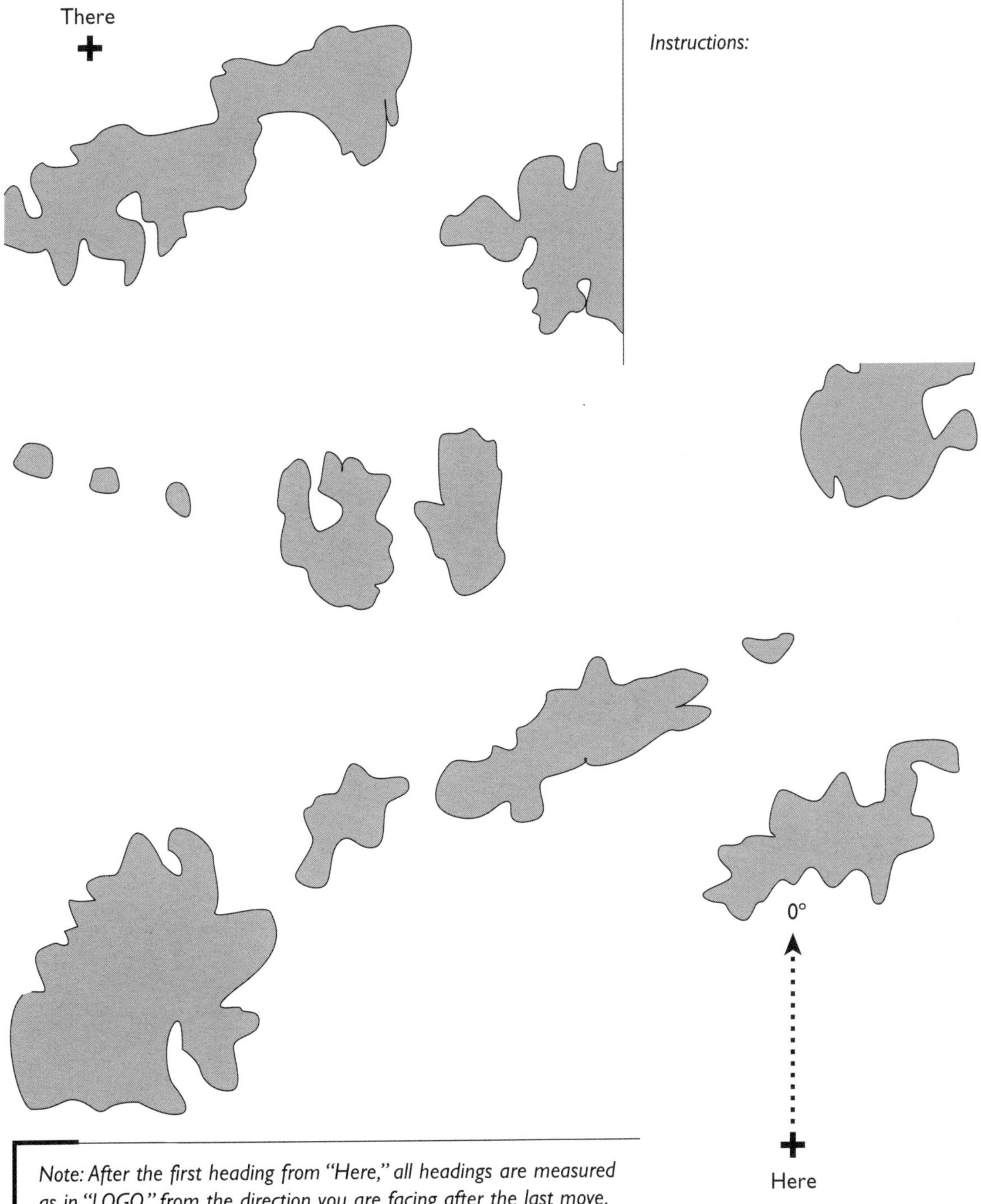

There

0°

Here

Note: After the first heading from "Here," all headings are measured as in "LOGO," from the direction you are facing after the last move.

NAVEGANDO EN LA OBSCURIDAD

Mapa—2

Curso escrito por:

Instrucciones:

Allá

0°

Aquí

Nota: Después de la primera orientación de «Aquí,» todas las orientaciones se miden como un «LOGO,» de la dirección en que te diriges después de la última movida.

NAVIGATING IN THE DARK

Map—3

Course written by:

Instructions:

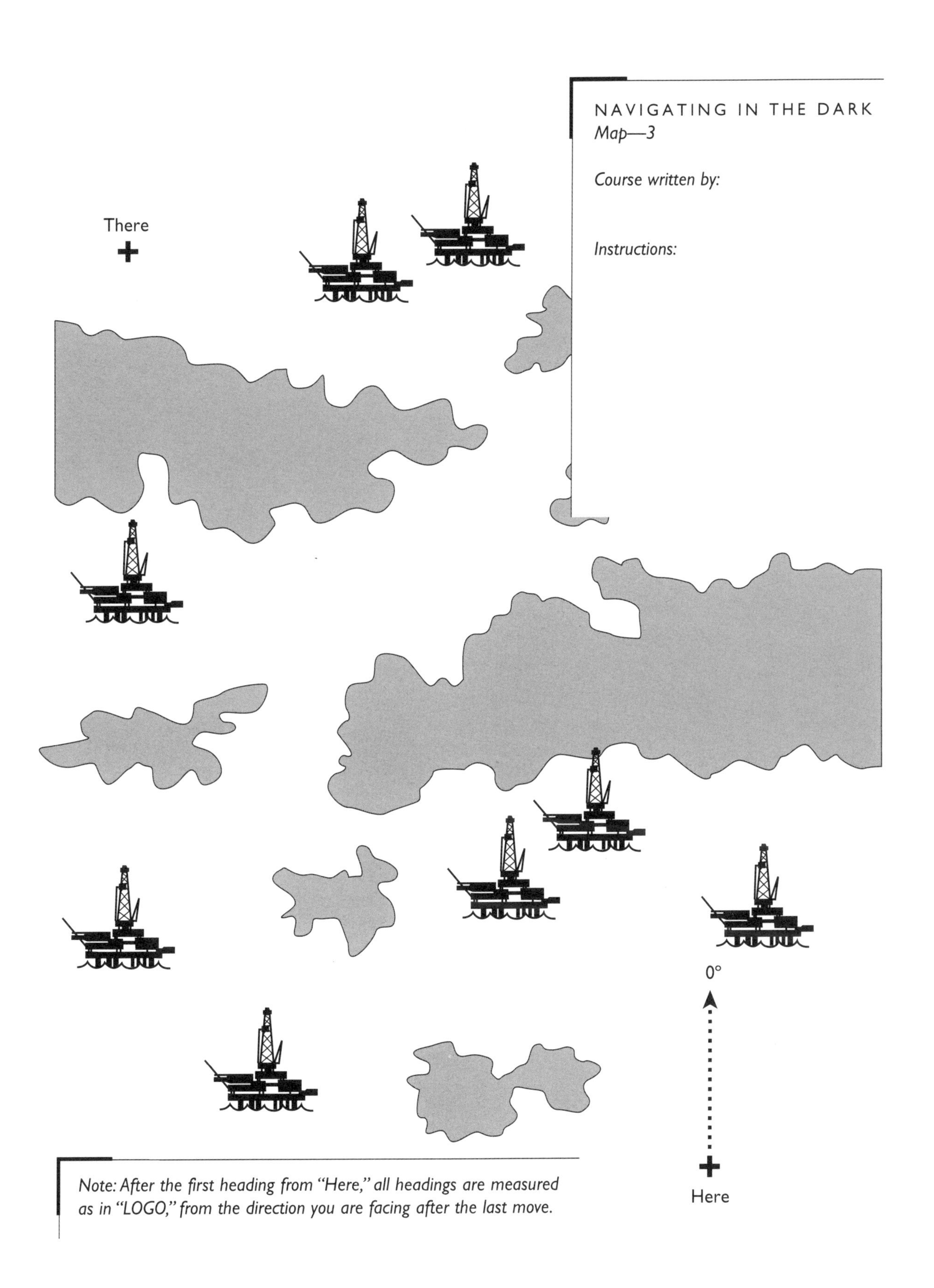

Note: After the first heading from "Here," all headings are measured as in "LOGO," from the direction you are facing after the last move.

NAVEGANDO EN LA OBSCURIDAD

Mapa—3

Curso escrito por:

Instrucciones:

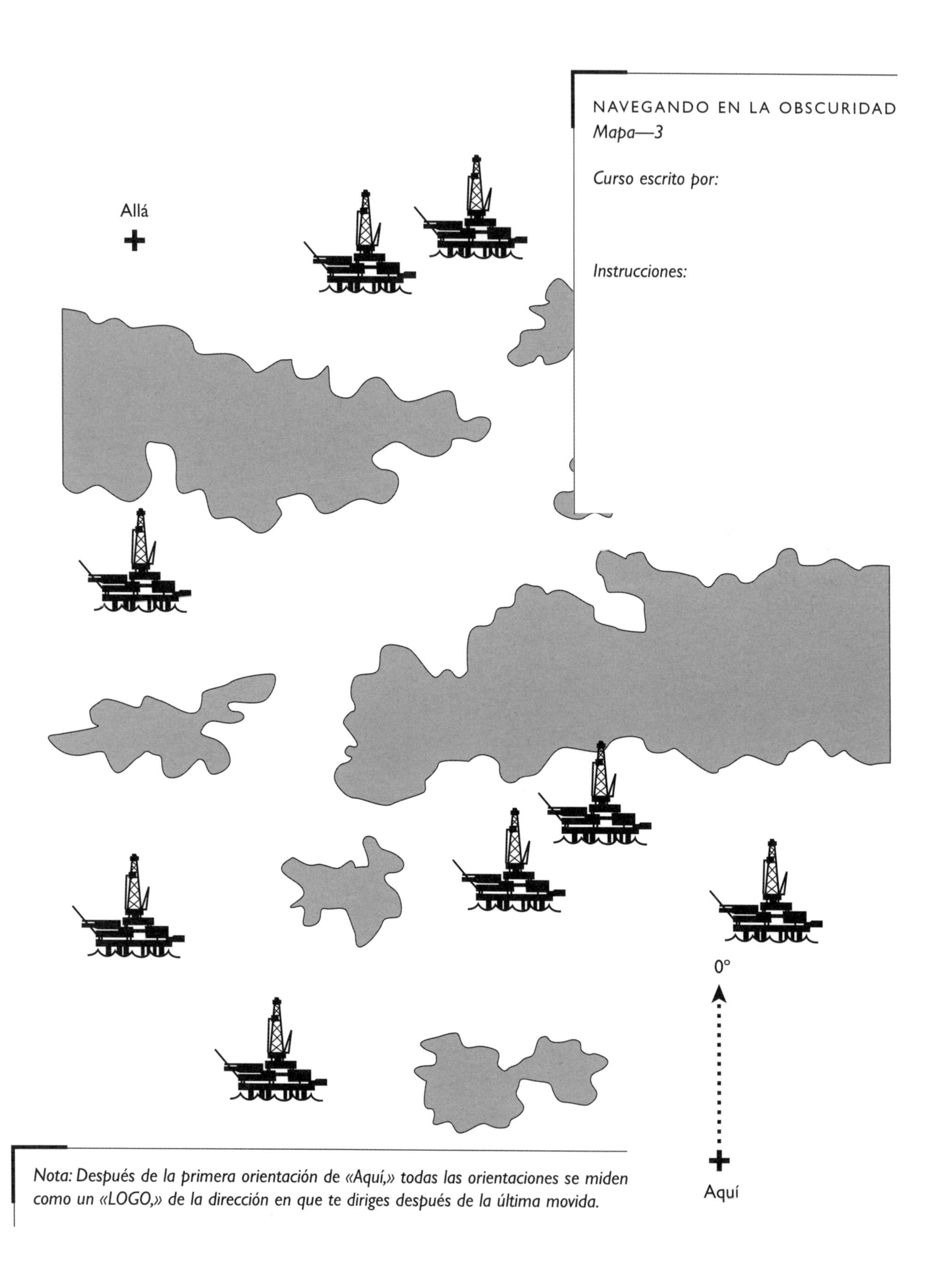

Nota: Después de la primera orientación de «Aquí,» todas las orientaciones se miden como un «LOGO,» de la dirección en que te diriges después de la última movida.

NAVIGATING IN THE DARK

Map—4

Course written by:

Instructions:

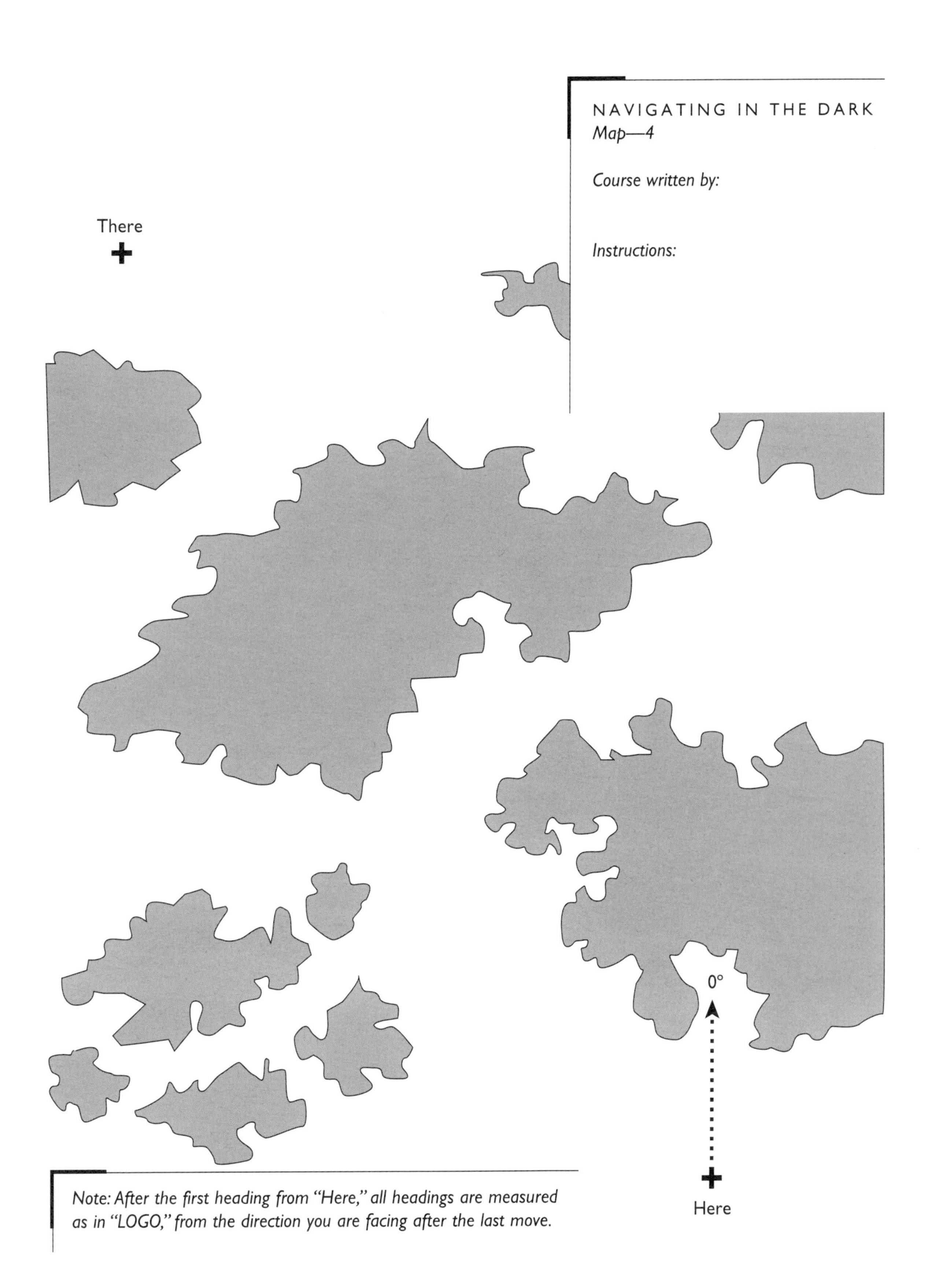

Note: After the first heading from "Here," all headings are measured as in "LOGO," from the direction you are facing after the last move.

NAVEGANDO EN LA OBSCURIDAD

Mapa—4

Curso escrito por:

Instrucciones:

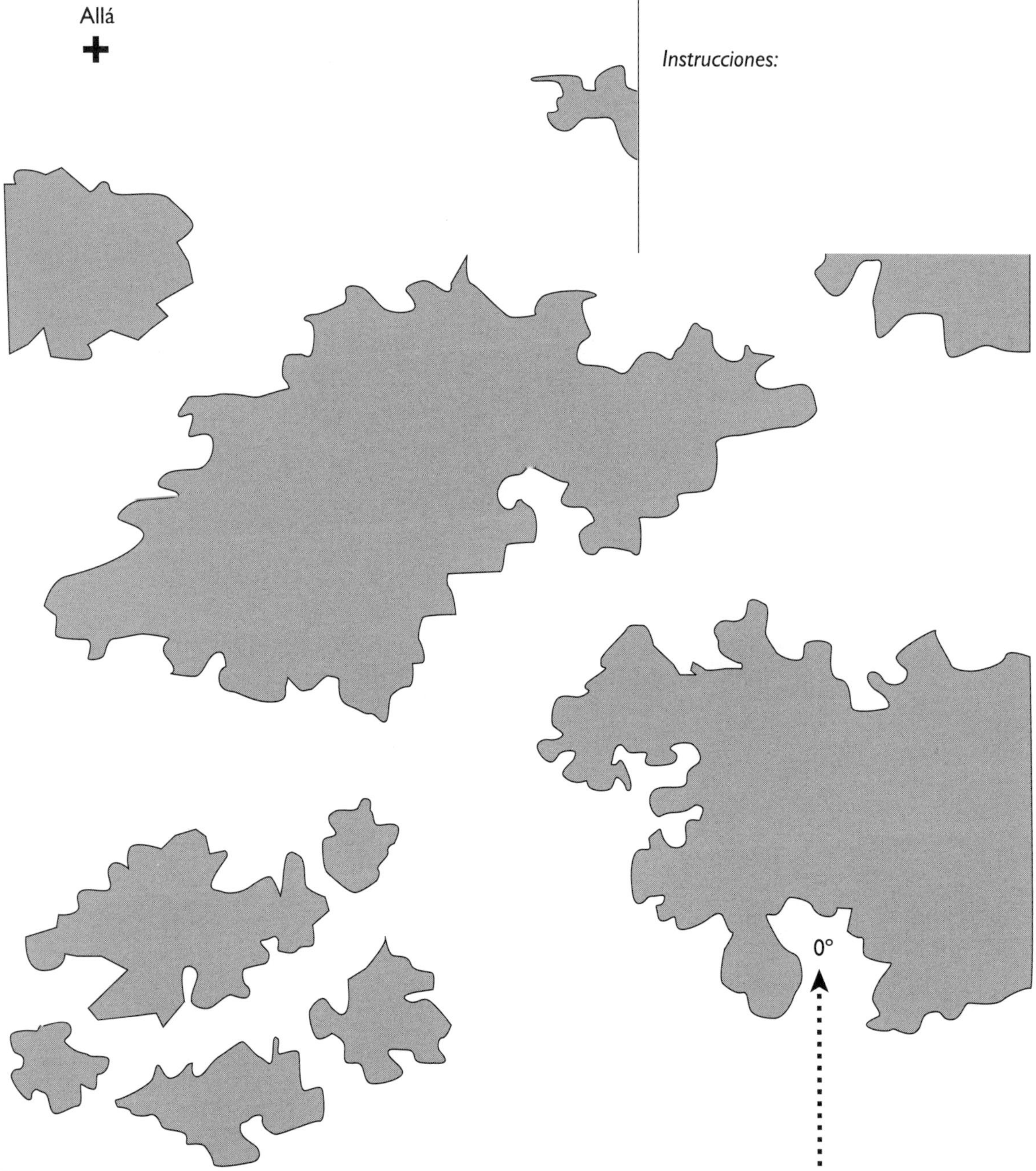

Allá

0°

Aquí

Nota: Después de la primera orientación de «Aquí,» todas las orientaciones se miden como un «LOGO,» de la dirección en que te diriges después de la última movida.

NAVIGATING IN THE DARK

Map—5

Course written by:

Instructions:

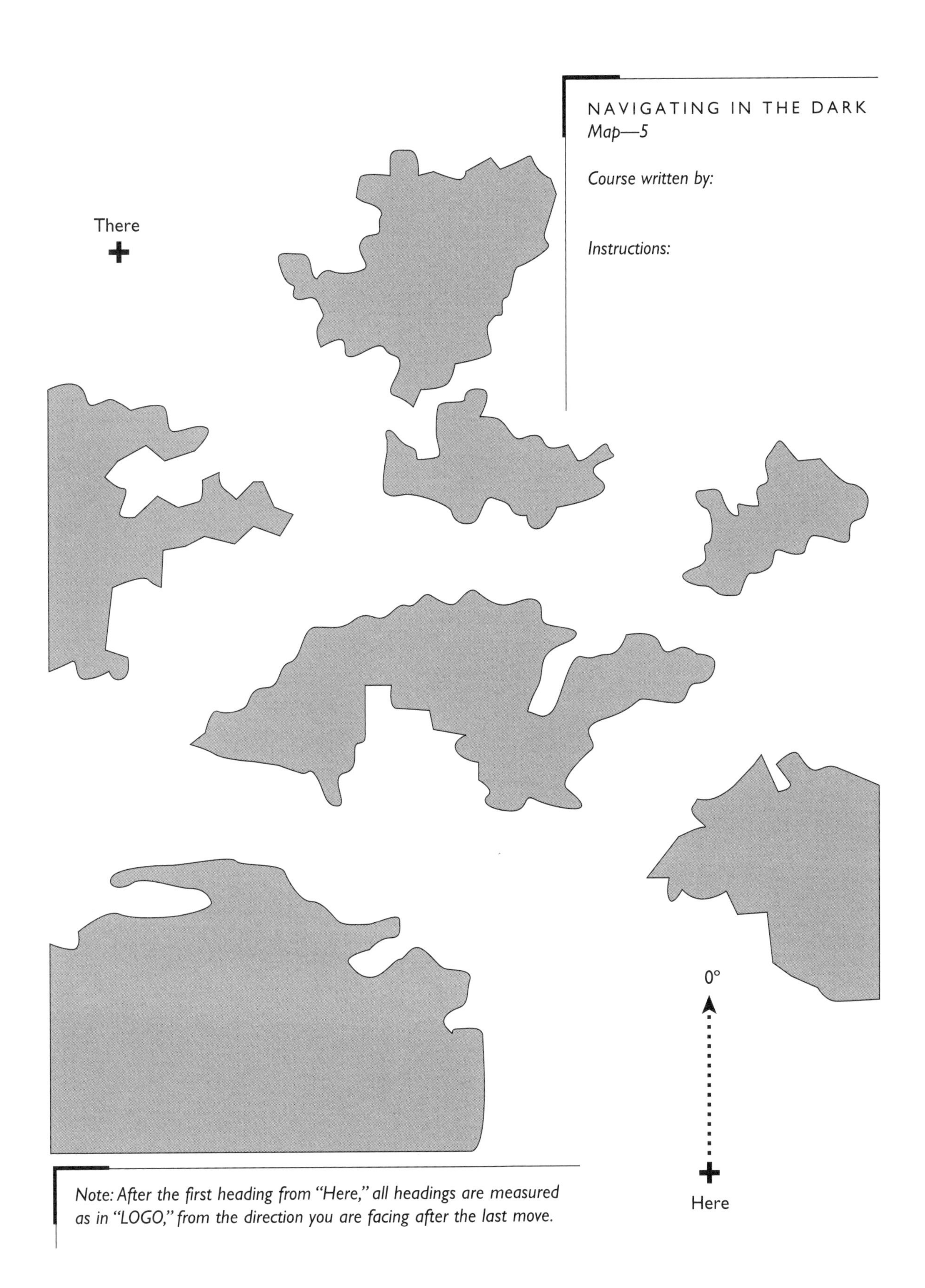

Note: After the first heading from "Here," all headings are measured as in "LOGO," from the direction you are facing after the last move.

NAVEGANDO EN LA OBSCURIDAD

Mapa—5

Curso escrito por:

Instrucciones:

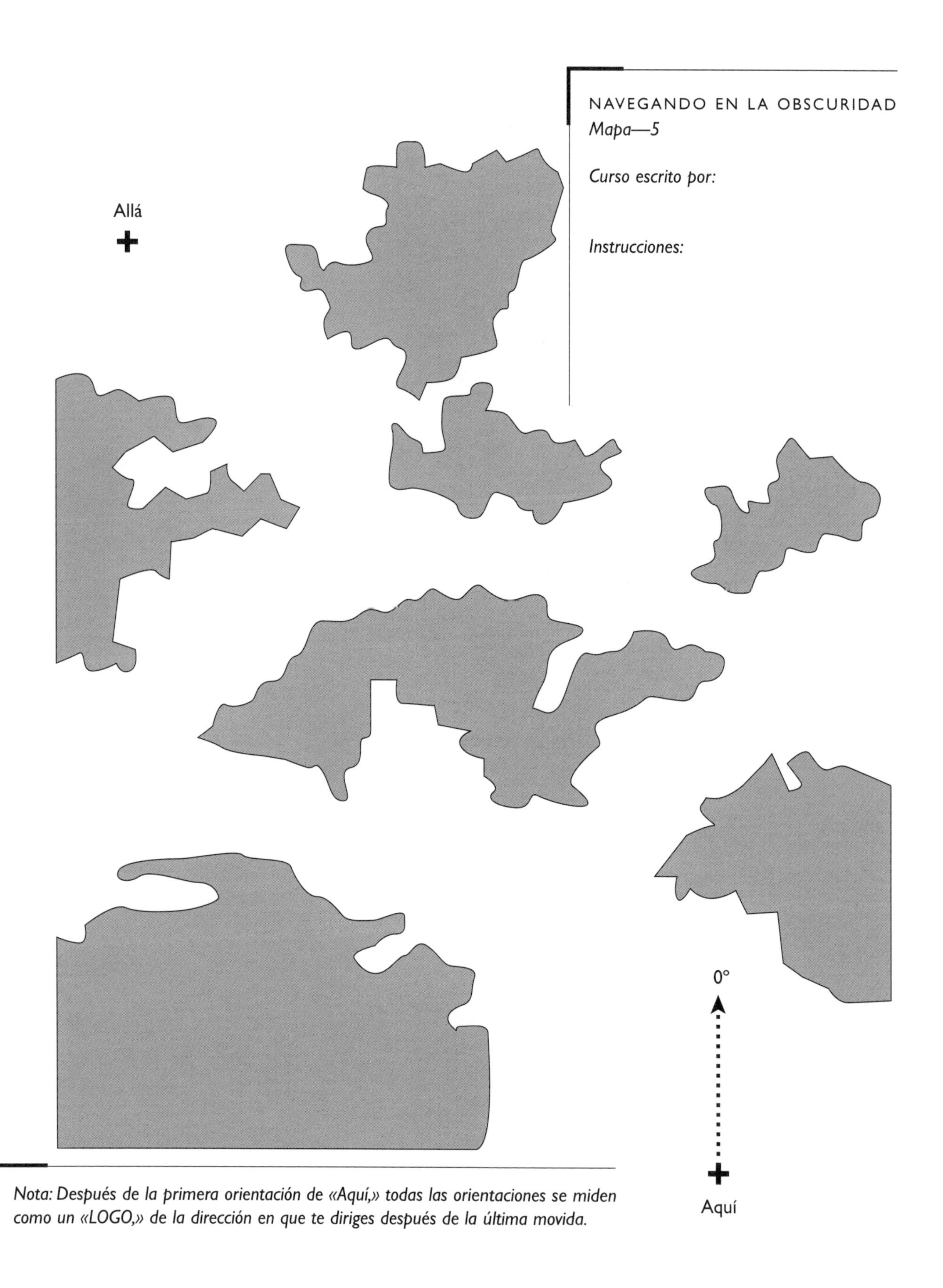

Nota: Después de la primera orientación de «Aquí,» todas las orientaciones se miden como un «LOGO,» de la dirección en que te diriges después de la última movida.

NAVIGATING IN THE DARK
Homework—Oil Tanker

Name:

Period:

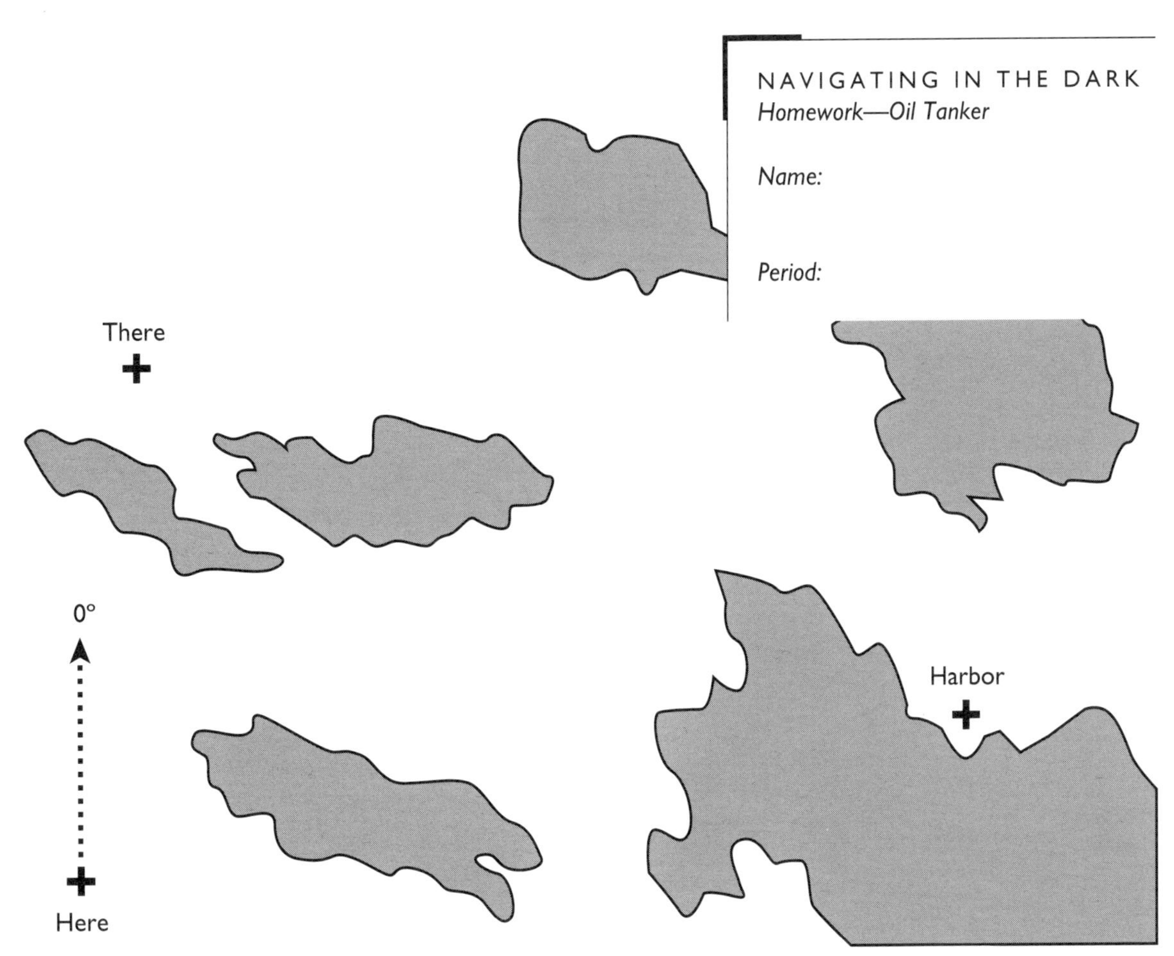

1) Plot a straight line course from "Here" to the Harbor and from the Harbor to "There." Measure the headings for each turn and the distances for each run. Check each direction to make sure it is accurate.

   Directions:

   ____

   ____

   ____

   ____

   ____

2) If 1 cm on this map represents 5 nautical miles, what is the total distance your ship travels?

   If your ship were traveling at a rate of 12 knots, how long would the trip take? Knots are the number of nautical miles per hour. A nautical mile is about 1.15 land, or statute, miles.

   Use the back of this sheet to explain how you got your answer and to show your work.

NAVEGANDO EN LA OBSCURIDAD

Tarea—Buque Petrolero

Nombre:

Período:

1) Delinea una raya derecha de «Aquí» hasta el Puerto y del Puerto hasta «Allá.» Mide las orientaciones para cada vuelta y la distancia de cada corrida. Verifica cada dirección para que estés seguro que sean precisas.

   Direcciones:

   ____

   ____

   ____

   ____

   ____

2) Si un centímetro de este mapa representa 5 millas náuticas, ¿cuál es la distancia total que tu barco recorre? Si tu barco estuviera recorriendo a una velocidad de 12 nudos, ¿cuánto tiempo duraría el viaje? Nudos son el número de millas náuticas por hora. Una milla náutica es más o menos 1.15 millas de tierra o de estatuto. Usa el reverso de ésta hoja para explicar cómo es que obtuviste tu respuesta y enseña todo tu trabajo.

Homework—Atolls

Name:

Period:

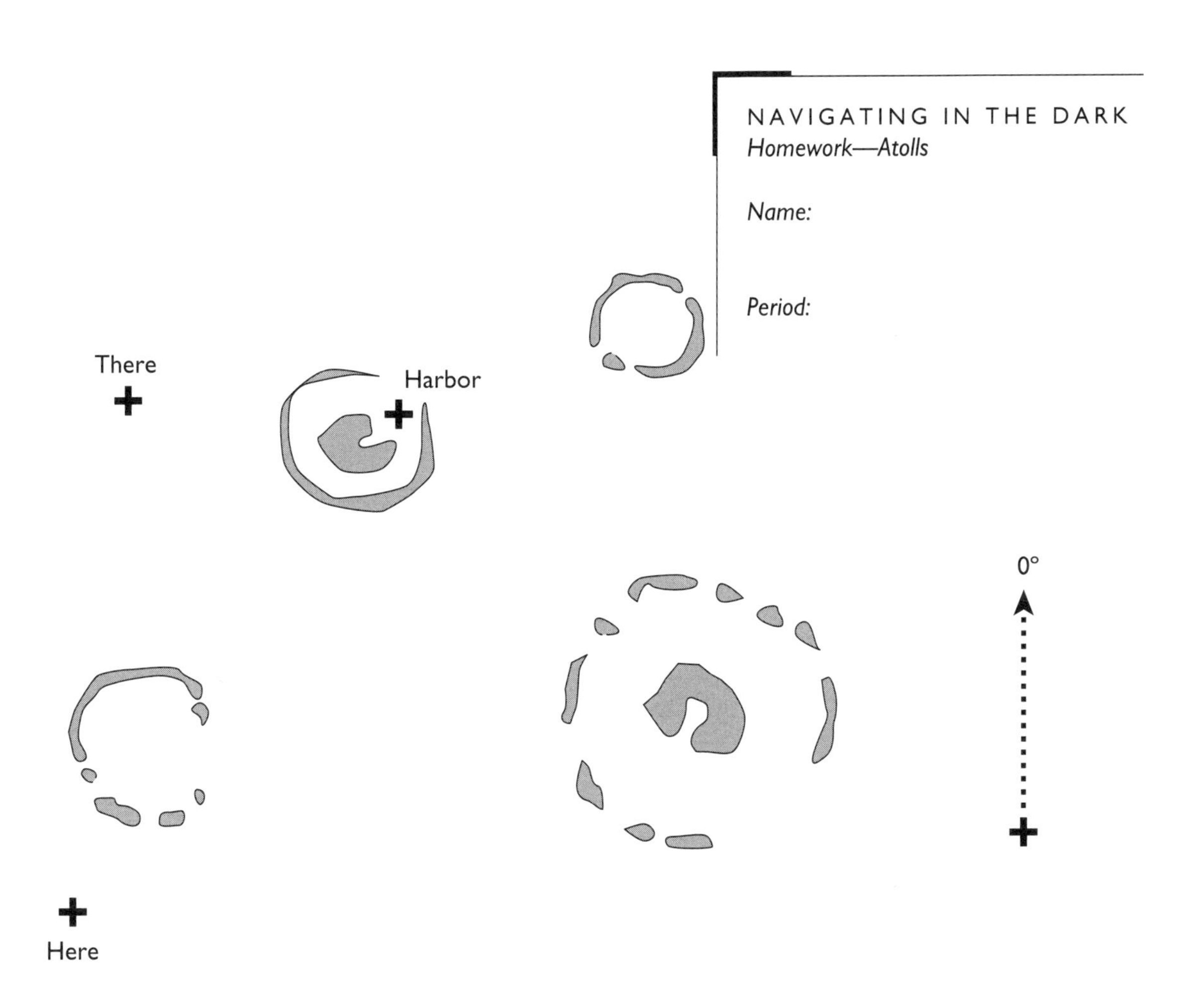

1) Plot a straight line course from "Here" to the Harbor and then from the Harbor to "There." Measure the headings for each turn and the distances for each run. Check each direction to make sure it is accurate.

   Directions:

   ___

   ___

   ___

   ___

   ___

2) Your tanker holds 38,000 tons of oil. Generally, there are about seven barrels to a ton; the exact number varies with the type of oil. A barrel is 42 gallons. How many gallons might you spill, if you were to run aground? Explain and show your work.

NAVEGANDO EN LA OBSCURIDAD
Tarea—Atolones

Nombre:

Período:

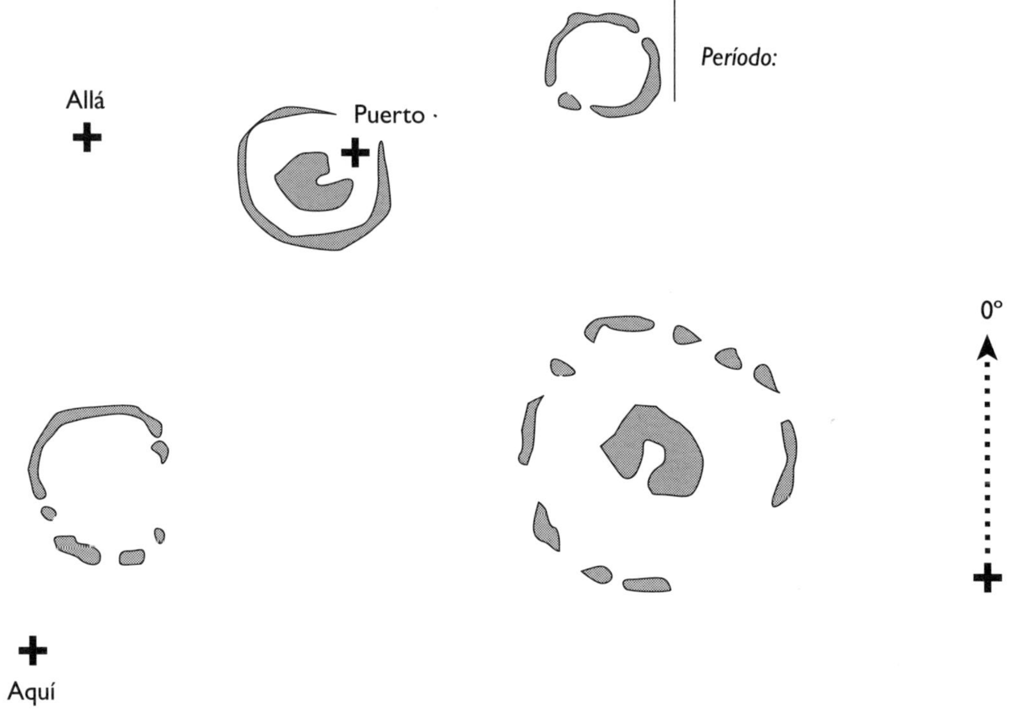

Allá

Puerto

0°

Aquí

1) Delinea una raya derecha de <<Aquí>> hasta el Puerto y del Puerto hasta <<Allí.>> Mide las orientaciones para cada vuelta y la distancia de cada corrida. Verifica cada dirección para que estés seguro que sean precisas.

   Direcciones:

   ____

   ____

   ____

   ____

   ____

2) Tu buque sostiene 38,000 toneladas de aceite. Generalmente, hay como siete barriles para cada tonelada; el número exacto varea con el tipo de aceite. Un barril equivale a 42 galones. ¿Cuántos galones puedes derramar, si fueras a encallarte? Explícalo y enseña tu trabajo.

Navigating in the Dark: Instructions for the Investigative Reporter

1. Place the Navigation Sheet over the original map to find any errors.
2. If there are places where the paths don't match, mark them and circle the instructions that match them.
3. Check all the measurements yourself to see where errors, if any, occurred.
4. Write a brief article reporting your findings. Tell exactly where the errors occurred. Be sensitive to and respectful of the novice course writers and captains.
5. Attach your article to the map and the Navigation sheets and return them to your teacher.

Navegando en la Obscuridad: Instrucciones para el Reportero Investigador

1. Coloca la Hoja de Navegación sobre el mapa original para encontrar errores.
2. Si hay lugares en donde los senderos no coinciden, anótalos, y circula las instrucciones que les corresponde.
3. Tú mismo/a revisa todas las medidas para ver en dónde ocurrieron, si es que ocurrieron.
4. Escribe un artículo breve reportando lo que averiguaste. Anota exactamente dónde ocurrieron los errores. Asegúrate de ser sensitivo/a y respetuoso/a de los escritores novicios del curso y los capitanes.
5. Junta el artículo con el mapa y las hojas de Navegación, y regrésaselas a tu maestro/a.

Navigating in the Dark
Navigational Masters Series

Written by______________________

Instructions:

____
____
____
____
____
____
____

Followed by
Name: Date:

____
____
____
____

Navigating in the Dark
Navigational Masters Series

Written by______________________

Instructions:

Followed by
Name: Date:

____
____
____
____
____
____
____
____
____
____
____

Navigating in the Dark
Navigational Masters Series

Written by______________________

Instructions:

Followed by
Name: Date:

____
____
____
____
____
____
____
____
____
____
____

Navegando en la Obscuridad
Series Principales de Navegación

Escrito por______________________

Instrucciones:

____
____
____
____
____
____
____

Seguido por
Nombre: Fecha:

____
____
____
____

Navegando en la Obscuridad
Series Principales de Navegación

Escrito por______________________

Instrucciones:

____
____
____
____
____
____
____

Seguido por
Nombre: Fecha:

____
____
____
____

Navegando en la Obscuridad
Series Principales de Navegación

Escrito por______________________

Instrucciones:

____
____
____
____
____
____
____

Seguido por
Nombre: Fecha:

____
____
____
____

Name ______________________________

Changes in Paths Resulting From Changes In Lengths

When navigation equipment is faulty or measurement tools are not precise, errors are compounded, especially when a path consists of several legs. To analyze errors, it is important to know how changes in directions affect paths navigated.

We will analyze the effects of two kinds of changes, adding and multiplying:

1. How does a path change if the length of each leg has some distance, such as 1.5 cm, added?

2. How does a path change if the length of each leg is multiplied by some number, such as 1.5?

Your assignment:

- Choose a four-legged path to be your original.
- Make the changes suggested in questions 1 and 2 and draw the new figures.
- Write up your findings, using your drawings and Ratio Checks as evidence.

Nombre ______________________________

Cambios en los Senderos como Resultado de los Cambios en las Longitudes

Cuando un equipo de navegación es defectuoso, o las herramientas de medidas no son precisas, ocurren errores, especialmente cuando un sendero consiste de varias piernas. Para analizar errores, es importante saber los diferentes efectos causados por los cambios en las direcciones de los senderos.

Analizaremos los efectos de dos tipos de cambios, sumando y multiplicando:

1.) ¿Cómo cambia un sendero si a las longitudes de todas las piernas se les suma alguna distancia, como 1.5 cm?

2.) ¿Cómo cambia un sendero si a las longitudes de todas las piernas son multiplicadas por algún número, como 1.5?

Tu tarea:

- Escoge un sendero de cuatro piernas para que sea tu "original".
- Haz dibujos nuevos para encontrar respuestas posibles a las preguntas 1 y 2.
- Escribe los resultados que encontraste, usando tus dibujos y la revisión de proporciones, como evidencia.

Name ____________________

Mathematics Toolkit

In your own words, write a definition for each term below and describe why it is useful. Give at least one example and include a sketch for each term:

- ANGLE CHECK

- SIMILAR SHAPES

- RATIO CHECK

Based on the Group Reports, what can you say about changes in paths when:

1) all legs of the original path have the same length added to them?

2) all legs of the original path are multiplied by the same number?

Nombre ______________________________

Estuche de Herramienta Matemática

En tus propias palabras, escribe el significado y la utilez de cada uno de los términos de abajo. Dá, por lo menos, un ejemplo incluyendo un esquema para cada uno de los términos:

- REVISION DEL ANGULO

- FIGURAS SIMILARES

- REVISION DE PROPORCIONES

Basándote en los Reportes del Grupo, qué puedes decir sobre los cambios en cada sendero cuando:

1) ¿a todas las piernas del sendero original, se les suma la misma longitud?

2) ¿a todas las piernas del sendero original se les multiplica el mismo número?

Paths For Group Investigations

Bow tie-shaped paths

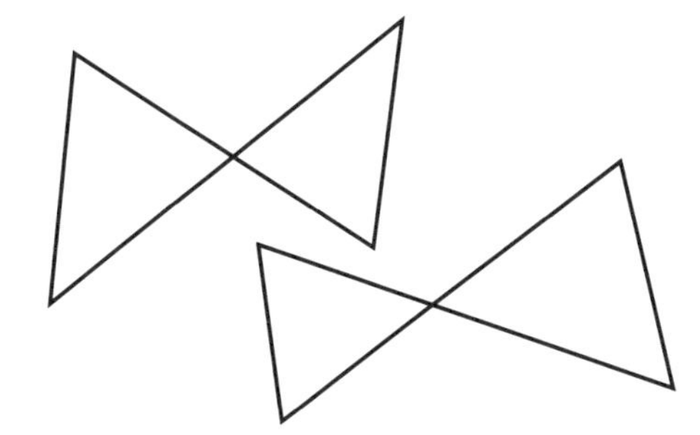

Boomerang-shaped paths (closed paths with four legs and shaped like a boomerang)

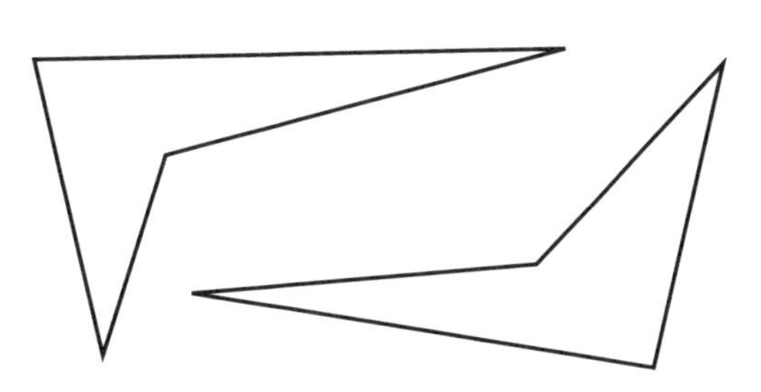

Paths with legs all of equal length

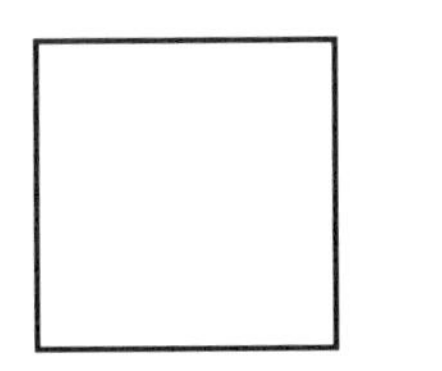

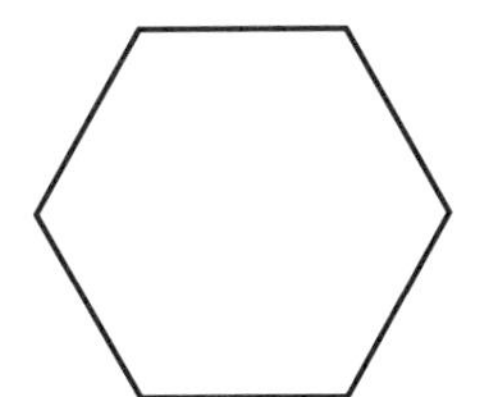

Rectangular-shaped paths

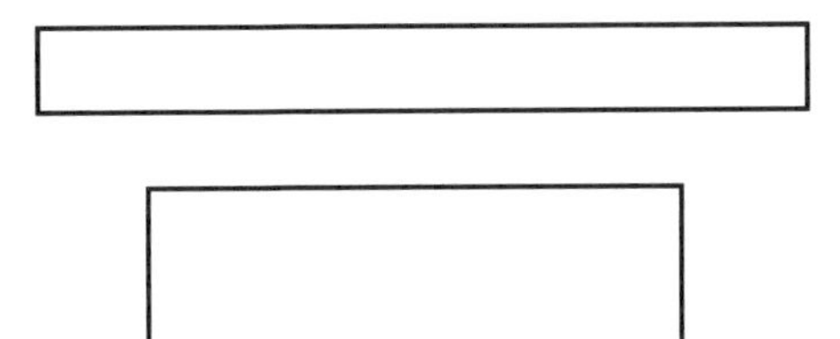

Closed, four-leg paths with no legs equal

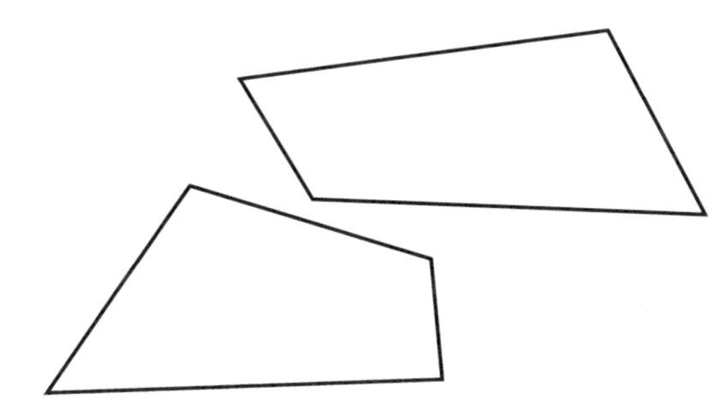

Kite-shaped paths (closed paths with four legs having two pairs of adjoining legs equal)

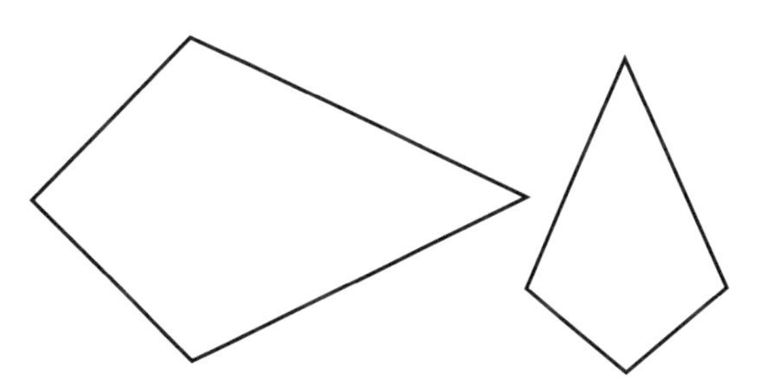

Triangular paths (closed paths with three legs)

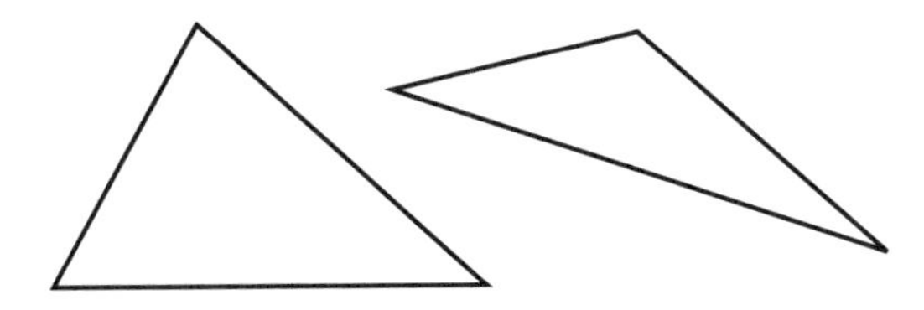

Closed paths with five or more legs

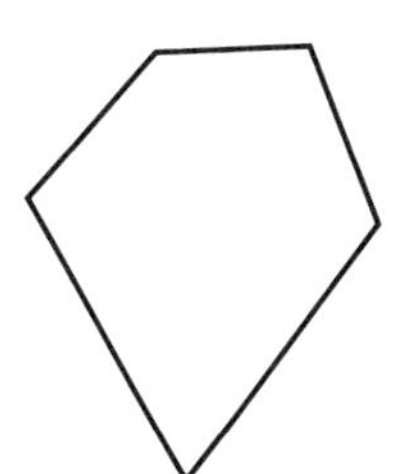

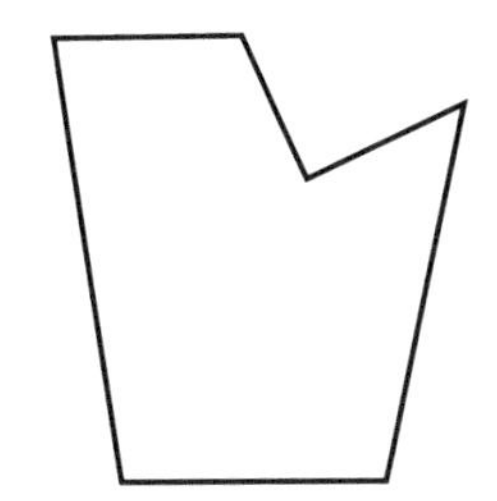

Senderos para las Investigaciones de Grupo

Senderos tipo corbata de lazo

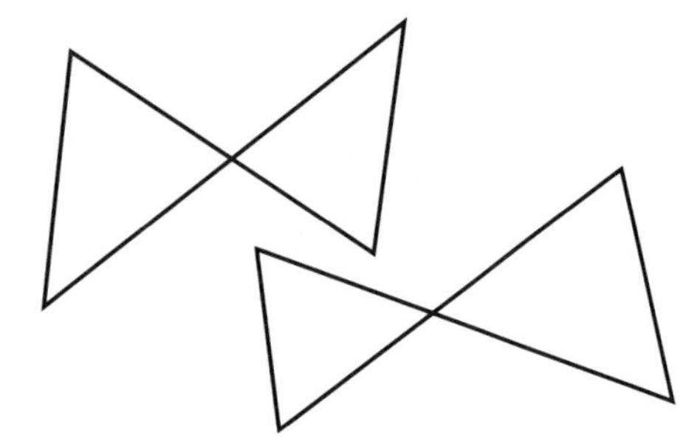

Senderos tipo bumerang (Senderos cerrados de cuatro piernas con forma de bumerang)

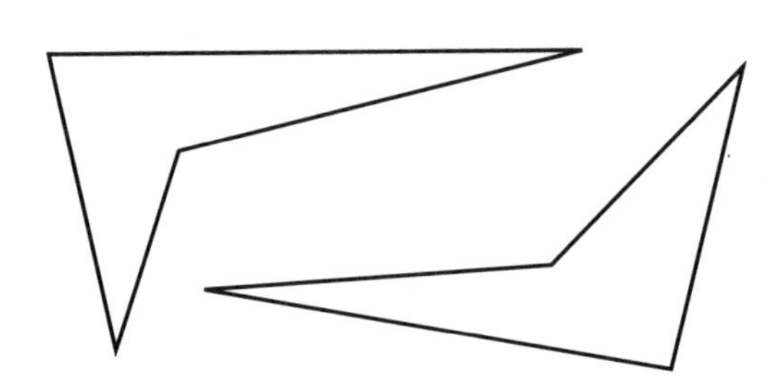

Senderos de cuatro piernas equivalentes

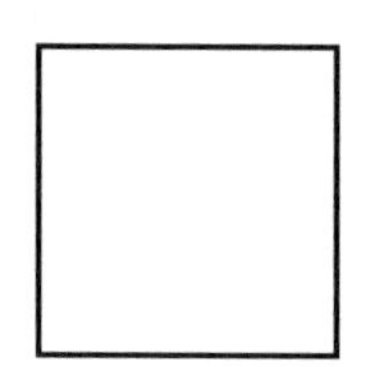

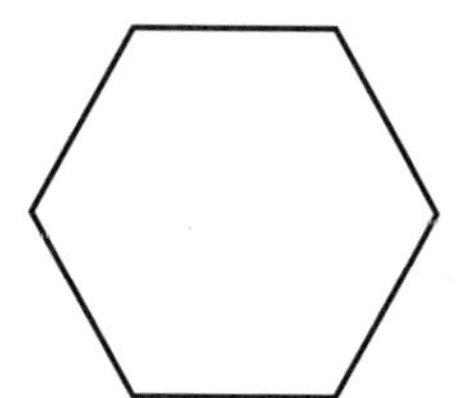

Senderos rectangulares

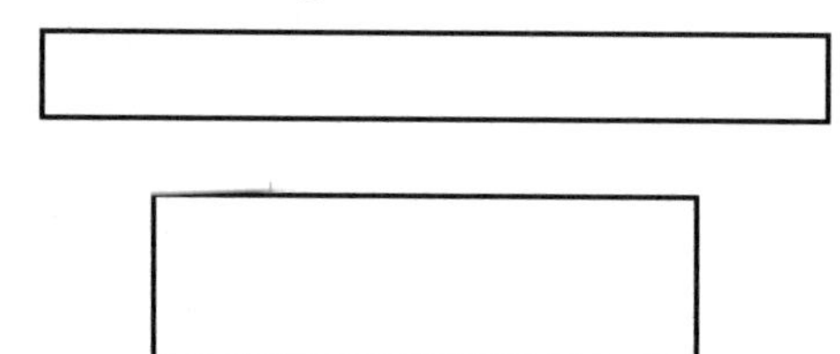

Senderos cerrados con cuatro piernas de tamaños diferentes

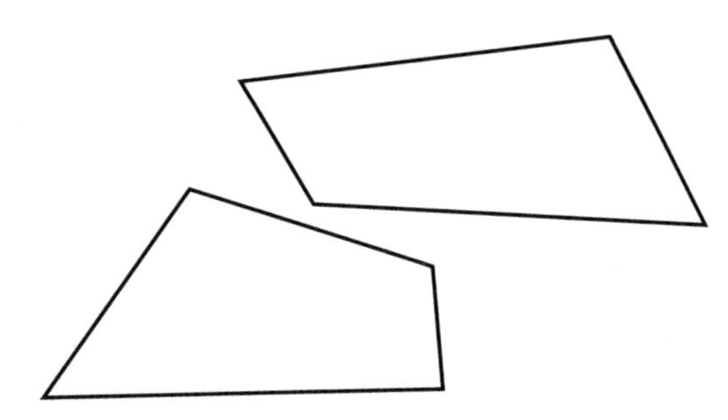

Senderos tipo papalote (Senderos cerrados de dos pares de piernas contiguas equivalentes)

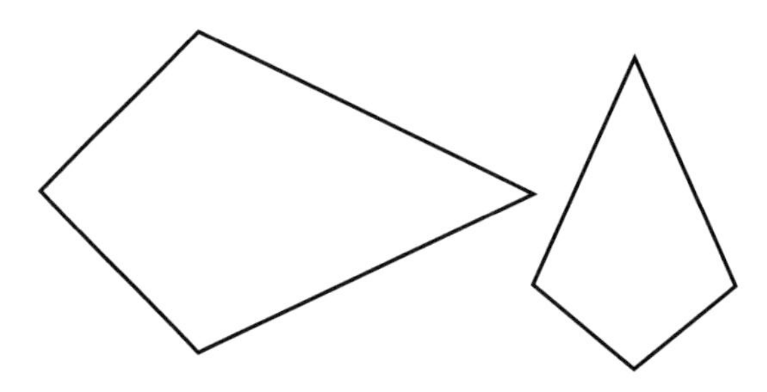

Senderos triangulares (Senderos cerrados de tres piernas)

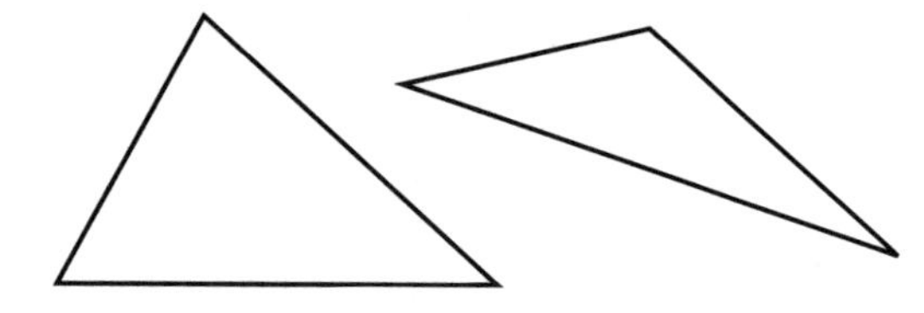

Senderos cerrados de cincos piernas o más

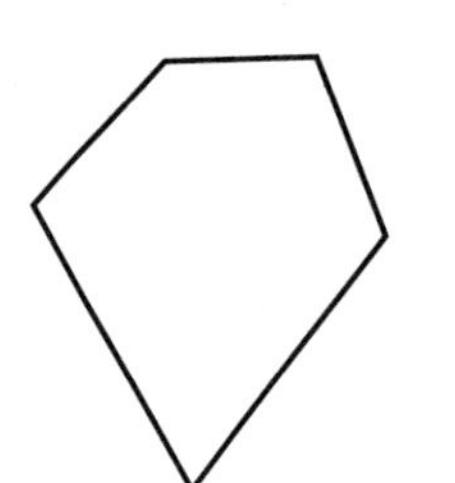

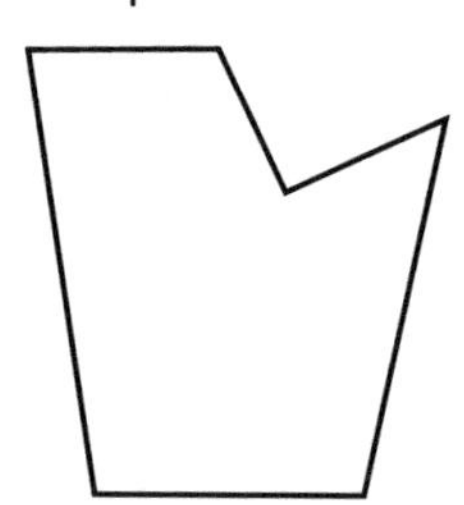

Names of group members:

____

____

Group Investigation Assignment

Path shape your group is assigned:

As a group, research and prepare an oral report for the class about your shape. Include answers to the three questions below.

What happens to any path if the same number is added to (or subtracted from) the length of each leg? Why?

What happens to any path if each leg of the path is multiplied or divided by the same number? Why?

Are there any kinds of paths that are exceptions to your findings?

Your report must include several accurate drawings as evidence to support your answers.

After all reports are complete, the class will compile the information and try to answer the three questions for paths of all shapes.

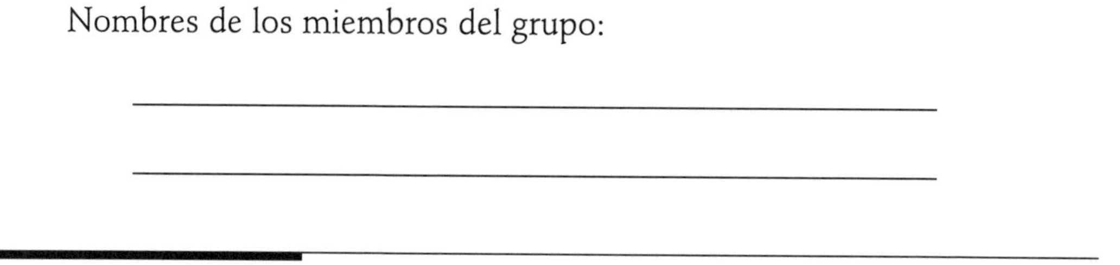

Tarea Para la Investigación del Grupo

Forma del sendero asignada a tu grupo:

Tu grupo debe llevar a cabo una investigación y preparar un reporte oral para la clase. Incluye respuestas para las tres preguntas de abajo.

¿Qué le ocurre a cualquier sendero, si el mismo número se le suma (o se le resta) a la longitud de cada pierna? ¿Por qué?

¿Qué le ocurre a cualquier sendero, si a cada pierna del sendero se le multiplica (o divide) por el mismo número? ¿Por qué?

¿Hay alguna clase especial de senderos que sea la excepción?

Tu reporte debe incluir varios dibujos precisos, como evidencia para apoyar tus respuestas.

Después de que todos los reportes estén completos, como una clase, juntos intentaremos contestar las tres preguntas en general para los senderos de todas las formas.

Step-by-Step Guide For Doing the Group Investigation

Your group may use the following steps as a guide to prepare your report:

■ MAKE THE ORIGINALS

- Draw at least two different paths with the shape your group has been assigned.
- Paths should be about the size of a hand.
- Label these drawings "Original #1" and "Original #2."
- Carefully measure the length and the heading for each leg.
- Write the instructions for drawing each path.

■ INVESTIGATE ADDITION

For each set of instructions for your original paths:

- Choose a number and add it to the length of each leg.
- Make a new drawing using these altered instructions.
- Describe how the new drawing compares to the original.

■ INVESTIGATE MULTIPLICATION

For each set of instructions for your original paths:

- Choose a number and multiply the length of each leg by it.
- Make a new drawing using these altered instructions.
- Describe how the new drawing compares to the original.

1. Make several drawings to help you reach conclusions about the overall effects addition and multiplication has on paths.
2. Make a poster displaying some of the drawings to show what happens.
3. Prepare an oral report of your findings.

Guía de Paso a Paso para Construir la Investigación de Grupo

Tu grupo puede usar los siguientes pasos como guía, en preparación para el reporte:

■ CONSTRUYE LOS ORIGINALES

- Dibuja, por lo menos, dos senderos diferentes con la forma que se le asignó a tu grupo.
- Los senderos deberían ser, más o menos, al tamaño de tu mano.
- Nombra estos dibujos «Original #1» y «Original #2».
- Con mucho cuidado, mide la longitud y la orientación para cada pierna.
- Escribe las instrucciones para dibujar cada sendero.

■ INVESTIGA LA ADICION

Para cada serie de instrucciones de tus senderos originales:

- Escoge un número y súmaselo a la longitud de cada pierna.
- Haz un dibujo nuevo usando las instrucciones.
- ¿Cómo se compara el dibujo nuevo con el original?

■ INVESTIGA LA MULTIPLICACION

Para cada serie de instrucciones de tús senderos originales:

- Escoge un número y multiplícaselo a la longitud de cada pierna.
- Haz un dibujo nuevo usando estas instrucciones modificadas.
- ¿Cómo se compara el dibujo nuevo con el original?

1. Haz varios dibujos para ayudarte averiguar conclusiones sobre los efectos de adición y multiplicación en los senderos.
2. Haz un letrero que enseñe algunos de los dibujos para demostrar lo que ocurre.
3. Prepara un reporte oral sobre tus resultados.

Everyone knows that accuracy and precision are important when orienteering, navigating, designing, or surveying. But errors sometimes happen. Some errors are due to mistakes that human beings make, like reading instruments incorrectly, or not sighting lengths or angles carefully. Some errors are due to faulty measuring tools.

■ YOUR ASSIGNMENT

You work for a company that manufactures precision orienteering instruments. A mistake was made in the design of two of the rulers your company produces. Thousands of these faulty rulers have already been shipped to customers. The company president decides to recall all the rulers and replace them, but this will take several months. To avoid a possible major suit and consequent loss of profit, she asks you to investigate the effects of faulty rulers using the different closed paths. She asks you to write a report on your findings and recommended modifications.

Your report, along with supporting diagrams, wlll be sent to customers to use until they receive the new rulers. Customers include the coach of an Olympic orienteering team, ship captains, navigational chart makers, students at several grade schools, engineers, designers, and many other professionals. You can choose to write your report to people in one or more of these professions to help them meet their special needs.

Here are the faulty rulers that need to be analyzed:

The Long Ruler

The Long Ruler has an extra amount of length between its "0" and "1" marks. The lengths between the other marks, between the "1" and the "2", the "2" and the "3", etc., are all accurate.

The Enlarged Ruler

The Enlarged Ruler looks like a normal ruler, but the distances among *all* the marks are 1.3 times as long as a normal ruler.

Proyecto de Investigación Individual: Analizando los Efectos de las Herramientas de Medir Defectuosas

Todos saben que la exactitud y la precisión son importante cuando uno orienta, navega, diseña, o agrimensura. Pero errores algunas veces suceden. Algunos son causados por errores humanos, como leer instrumentos incorrectamente, o no apuntando longitudes o ángulos cuidadosamente. Algunos errores son a causa de herramientas de medir defectuosas.

■ TU TAREA

Trabajas para una compañía que manufactura instrumentos de precisión orientada. Un error fue hecho en el diseño de las dos reglas que tu compañía produce. Miles de estas reglas defectuosas ya se han enviado a los clientes. El presidente de la compañía decide retirar todas la reglas y reemplazarlas, pero ésto tomará muchos meses. Para evitar una posible demanda y una consecuente pérdida de ganancia, ella te pide que investigues los efectos de las reglas defectuosas, usando los diferentes senderos cerrados. Te pide que escribas un reporte sobre tus descubrimientos y sobre tus modificaciones recomendadas.

Tu reporte, junto con diagramas que lo apoyen, serán enviados a los clientes para que los usen hasta que reciban las nuevas reglas. Los clientes incluyen el entrenador de un equipo Olímpico de Orientación, Capitanes de barcos, marcadores de mapas de navegación, estudiantes en diferentes primarias, ingenieros, diseñadores, y muchos otros profesionales. Puedes escojer escribir tu reporte a personas en una o más de éstas profesiones para ayudarles a encontrar sus necesidades especiales.

Aquí están las reglas defectuosas que deben ser analizadas:

La Regla Larga

La Regla Larga tiene una longitud adicional entre sus marcadores «0» y «1». La longitud entre los otros marcadores, entre el «1» y «2», y los marcadores «2» y «3», etc., son todos exactos.

La Regla Agrandada

La Regla Agrandada se ve como una regla normal, pero la distancia entre *todos* los marcadores son 1.3 más que una regla normal.

Names ______________________ ___________________________

Date ______________________ Period ______________________

Individual Investigation Self-Evaluation

The individual investigation is your opportunity to show what you have learned in this unit. Check the spaces as you complete them.

■ DIAGRAMS OF FAULTY TOOLS:

Long Ruler ________________________________ ____________

Enlarged Ruler ____________________________ ____________

■ A VARIETY OF CLOSED PATHS (CIRCLE AT LEAST FOUR SHAPES):

Square Rectangle Rhombus Trapezoid "Bow-tie"
Four unequal legs Boomerang Parallelogram
Other_____________

How many diagrams did you use to show what happens for each tool?:

Regular Ruler_____ Long Ruler____ Enlarged Ruler_____

For each drawing do you have

headings and directions?	Yes______	No ______	Some ______
angle accuracy check?	Yes______	No ______	Some ______
ratio check?	Yes______	No ______	Some ______

■ IN THE INTRODUCTION DID YOU: CHECK

write as if the audience were
the company president or_____________ ____________

state the purpose of the report ____________

describe the ruler with the extra
space length between 0 and 1 ____________

describe the ruler that is enlarged by some percent ____________

Nombre _______________ _______________
Fecha _______________ Período _______________

Evaluación Propia del Proyecto Individual

El proyecto individual es tu oportunidad de hacerle saber a tu maestro/a lo que haz aprendido en ésta unidad. Marca los espacios conforme hayas terminado las secciones.

▪ PROTOTIPOS DE HERRAMIENTAS DEFECTUOSAS:

Regla Larga _______________ _______
Regla Agrandada _______________ _______

▪ VARIEDAD DE LOS SENDEROS CERRADOS (CIRCULA POR LO MENOS CUATRO FIGURAS):

Cuadrado Rectángulo Rombo Trapezoide «Corbata de Lazo»
Cuatro Piernas Desiguales Bumerang Paralelogramo
Otro_____

¿Cuántos diagramas usaste para mostrar lo que pasa con cada herramienta?

Regla Regular______ Regla Larga______ Regla Agrandada______

¿Para cada dibujo tienes

orientaciones y direcciones? Sí_______No_______Algo_______
exactitud de ángulo? Sí_______No_______Algo_______
verificación de proporción? Sí_______No_______Algo_______

▪ EN LA INTRODUCCION: MARCA

escribiste como si la audencia fuera el presidente/a de una compañía o _______. _______
estableciste el propósito de tu reporte. _______
describiste la regla con el espacio extra con una longitud entre 0 y 1. _______
describiste la regla agrandada por un cierto porcentaje. _______

■ IN THE WRITTEN REPORT DID YOU:

include a detailed explanation of the effects of using each ruler to draw closed paths, and why those effects occurred.

Long Ruler ______ Enlarged Ruler ______

■ SAMPLE ORGANIZATION:

Title page. . . . . ________
Table of Contents . . . . ________
Introduction. . . . . ________
Written Report. . . . . ________
Warnings- Effects of Tools. . . . . ________

■ HOW WELL DO YOU THINK YOUR WORK ON THIS PROJECT SHOWS WHAT YOU LEARNED IN THIS UNIT?

■ HOW SATISFIED ARE YOU WITH YOUR WORK ON THIS PROJECT?

This is . . . (circle one):

My best work ever   Good work for me   Average work for me

Not up to my usual standards

■ EN EL REPORTE ESCRITO:

incluyiste una explicación detallada de los efectos de cada regla en los senderos cerrados, y por qué ocurrieron esos efectos .

Regla Larga______ Regla Agrandada______

■ EJEMPLO DE ORGANIZACION:

Portada ....____________
Tabla de Contenido ....____________
Introducción ....____________
Reporte Escrito. ....____________
Advertencias - Efectos de la Herramienta ....____________

■ ¿QUE TAN BIEN CREES QUE TU TRABAJO EN ESTE PROYECTO DEMUESTRE LO QUE HAYAS APRENDIDO EN ESTA UNIDAD?

■ ¿QUE TAN SATISFECHO/A TE SIENTES CON TU TRABAJO EN ESTE PROYECTO? (CIRCULA UNO):

Fue mi mejor trabajo Buen trabajo para mi

Trabajo regular para mi No fue mi mejor trabajo

Individual Investigation Seminar Questions

1. Find an example of a project that was organized clearly. Describe the format and explain why you think it is clear.
2. Find an example of high quality diagrams that show clearly how the shapes of paths changed when drawn with the faulty instruments.
3. Find an example of a true generalization that clearly states the effects of using one of the faulty instruments.
4. Find a report written to customers in a particular profession.
5. Find something that you learned from reading another student's project that you didn't know before.
6. Select another student's project that you liked and tell why.

Preguntas Seminarias del Proyecto Individual

1. Busca un ejemplo de un proyecto organizado claramente. Describe el formato y explica por qué crees que es claro.
2. Busca un ejemplo de diagramas de alta calidad que demuestren claramente cómo las formas de los senderos cambian cuando se dibujan con instrumentos defectuosos.
3. Busca un ejemplo de una generalización verdadera que claramente muestre los efectos en usar instrumentos defectuosos.
4. Busca un reporte escrito para clientes en una profesión particular.
5. Describe algo que aprendiste al leer el proyecto de otro estudiante que no hayas sabido antes.
6. Selecciona el proyecto de otro estudiante que te haya gustado e indica por qué te gustó.

Telling Someone Where To Go End-Of-Unit Assessment

1. Write a letter to a seventh grader explaining how to use a protractor to measure and lay out angles.
2. Explain what a *Ratio Check* is and what it is used for.
3. Draw a path shaped like a bow tie. Measure and write the instructions so another person could draw it without seeing it.
4. Mark a starting point and accurately draw this path:

   1) 0°, go 6.6 cm

   2) Left 120°, go 8.4 cm

   3) Right 130°, go 6.0 cm

   Find the distance and heading that will return you to the starting point.
5. Here are the turns for a closed orienteering path with four legs:

   0°, Right 123°, Left 97°, Left 108°

   Walk this path back to its starting point. Find the amount of turn needed to return you to the exact same direction you started.
6. Describe what did you liked best/least about the *Telling Someone Where To Go* unit.
7. Describe what you would recommend for this unit regarding improvements or changes.
8. Write a good question that you think belongs on this assessment and answer it.

1. Escríbele una carta a un estudiante del séptimo grado explicándole cómo usar un transportador para medir y construir ángulos.
2. Explícale qué es una *Revisión de Proporciones* y dile para qué se utiliza.
3. Dibuja un sendero tipo corbata de lazo. Mide y escribe las instrucciones para que otra persona los pueda dibujar sin verlo.
4. Marca un punto de partida y dibuja correctamente este sendero:

   1) Da vuelta 0°, camina 6.6 cm.

   2) Da vuelta 120° a la izquierda, camina 8.4 cm.

   3) Da vuelta 130° a la derecha, camina 6.0 cm.

   ¿Qué distancia y orientación te regresará al punto de partida?
5. Aquí están las vueltas para un sendero de orientación cerrado con cuatro piernas:

   0°, 123° a la derecha, 97° a la izquierda, 108° a la izquierda

   Camina este sendero hasta regresar a tu punto de partida. ¿Qué número de vueltas necesitas hacer para terminar exactamente en la misma dirección que empezaste?
6. Describe lo que te gustó más/menos sobre la unidad, *Diciéndole a Alguien a Dónde Ir.*
7. Describe los mejoramientos o cambios que recomendarías para ésta unidad.
8. Escribe una pregunta que creas que pertenezca en ésta evaluación y contéstala.

Judging Quality—Rubrics for Investigations Units

A rubric is a description of varying levels of success in accomplishing a task. Rubrics come in many versions, and can serve many purposes. Their usefulness is mostly in helping us (students and teachers) anticipate what good work will look like and evaluate whether the work we are looking at or have done is the best it can be.

Revision:

"The best it can be" should always direct us. The intent of a rubric should not be to label the student or the student's work, but to inform us of any additional effort needed to improve the product. The opportunity to revise is vital in helping students acquire the habit of persisting until they have done their best work.

In the following rubric suggestions you will find the terms "Ready for revision" and "Reteach." These should be taken to mean what they say. If work is not acceptable, suggestions and guidance should be provided that lead to successful revision. If the work indicates need for reteaching, that should be provided.

Student Participation:

Ideally, students will participate in creating a rubric by which their work can be evaluated. When they have practiced defining and applying high standards to their own and others' work, their chances for success increase.

Teacher input will be needed at some points, but we urge you to involve students to the maximum extent possible. The rewards can be amazing.

Levels:

In general, rubrics in current use in mathematics education have from two to six levels. The two-level rubric, of course, is a simple "Pass, No Pass" version. Others are more complex, and the choice of number of levels usually depends on the degree of distinguishing detail desired.

Ready-made Rubric:

On the following page is a prepared four-level rubric that describes characteristics for mathematical work, processes used, and presentation of a report. The italicized portions apply especially to this particular investigation, while the non-italicized parts constitute a generalized rubric.

The prepared rubric on the following page may give you and your students some starting ideas, but, as stressed above, we urge that you work together to create your own class rubrics.

Criterio para determinar la calidad- Rúbricas para las unidades Investigaciones

Una rúbrica es la descripción de los varios niveles de éxito en llevar a cabo una tarea. Hay rúbricas de diferentes formas que sirven varios propósitos. Las ventajas en usarlas son para ayudarnos (estudiantes y maestros) para anticipar cómo se parecerá el trabajo excelente y evaluar si la tarea que observamos o que hemos hecho está en la mejor forma posible.

Revisión

Siempre debemos dirigirnos a «la mejor forma posible». El intento de una rúbrica no debe ser para clasificar al estudiante ni su habilidad, sino para informarnos de los esfuerzos necesarios para mejorar el producto. La oportunidad para revisar es vital en ayudarle a los estudiantes para adquirir la costumbre de persistir hasta que hayan producido su mejor trabajo.

En las siguientes sugerencias para rúbricas, encontrarán los términos «Listo para revisión» y «Enseñar de nuevo». Estos indican que si la tarea no es aceptable, será necesario proveer sugerencias y direcciones que resultarán en revisión con buen resultado. En algunos casos será necesario enseñar de nuevo, para clarificar las instrucciones o los conceptos.

Participación del estudiante

Idealmente, los estudiantes participarán en crear la rúbrica por lo cual sus tareas puedan ser evaluadas. Cuando hayan practicado cómo definir y aplicar los criterios de calidad a su propia tarea y la de otros, las posibilidades de tener éxito aumentarán.

Aunque el profesor tendrá que contribuir ideas o guiar el trabajo en algunos puntos, recomendamos que involucren a los estudiantes a lo más que puedan. Los resultados pueden ser asombrosos.

Niveles

En general, las rúbricas que se usan en la educación matemática actualmente, tienen de dos a seis niveles. Una rúbrica de dos niveles, por supuesto, es una versión simple de «Aprobado, Desaprobado.» Otras son más complejas, y la selección del número de niveles depende en el grado de los distinguidos detalles deseados.

Ejemplo de una Rúbrica

En la página siguiente hay una rúbrica de cuatro niveles que describe las características matemáticas, los procesos usados, y la presentación de un reporte. Las porciones en letra itálica pertenecen especialmente a ésta investigación, mientras que las partes que no están escritas en letra itálica constituyen una rúbrica general.

La rúbrica preparada en la página siguiente les dará a usted y a sus estudiantes ideas para comenzar, pero recomendamos que trabajen junto con sus estudiantes para crear una rúbrica para su propio salón.

Telling Someone Where to Go—Judging Quality

	MATHEMATICS CONTENT	PROCESSES	PRESENTATION OF REPORT
WELL DONE	*There is careful analysis for faulty rulers.* *Effects on at least 4 different closed paths are compared.* *Each path is drawn correctly from accurate instructions, then shown as it would appear when drawn using a faulty measuring tool.* Mathematics is careful, accurate, and appropriate. Many or all possible variations are considered. Multiple representations (diagrams, words, formulas, etc.) are used. Analysis is thorough.	*Closed paths used are different shapes chosen from among the shapes class explored.* *Includes written generalization of the effect each tool would have on closed paths.* *Describes what happens to specific kinds of paths such as squares, "bow-ties," or symmetrical paths.* All work is completed. There is thoughtful organization (of data, information, presentations, etc.). Generalizations are made.	Written report is well-organized. Language is clear and appropriate (complete, understandable sentences). Format is neat and orderly. Appropriate audience is addressed.
ACCEPTABLE	Mathematics is generally careful and accurate, but with some errors in the work or in the logic applied. Limited number of possible variations are considered. Single representation is used. Analysis may need more care.	Organization may need to be improved. All work is completed. Recommendations may not relate completely to results or findings. Generalizations and predictions or further questions may be missing.	Language is generally clear and complete. Work is accurate and neat. Audience may not be clearly defined. Sources of information may not be complete.
READY FOR REVISION	Work may be the beginning of an acceptable report, but mathematics needs careful review and correction or refining.	The processes used should be reviewed and amended as needed. Focus questions from the teacher will lead to revisions.	Report provides a start but needs major revisions.
RESTART /RETEACH	Quality of work needs improvement or the topic is not useful—the project needs to be started over with further instruction.	More instruction is needed to find processes that will work for this investigation.	Report needs more direction in applying format, language, or other standards.

Diciéndole a Alguien a Dónde Ir—Criterio para Determinar la Calidad

	CONTENIDO MATEMÁTICO	PROCESOS	PRESENTACIÓN DE REPORTE
BIEN HECHO	*Hay análisis cuidadosa para las reglas defectuosas.* *Los efectos, en por lo menos cuatro diferentes senderos cerrados, están comparados.* *Cada sendero está dibujado correctamente usando instrucciones exactas, entonces está mostrado como si hubiera usado herramientas defectuosas de medir.* Las matemáticas son cuidadosas, exactas, y apropiadas. Consideró muchas o todas las variaciones posibles. Usa múltiples representaciones (como diagramas, palabras, fórmulas, etc.) El análisis es completo.	*Los senderos cerrados son de diferentes formas seleccionadas de las cuales usaron en la clase.* *Incluye una generalización escrita del efecto cada herramienta tendría en los senderos cerrados.* *Describe lo que ocurre a ciertas clases de senderos como los cuadrados, tipo corbata de lazo, o senderos simétricos.* Todo el trabajo está completo. Hay organización pensativa (del dato, información, presentaciones, etc.) Hace generalizaciones.	El reporte escrito está bien organizado. El lenguaje es claro y apropiado (oraciones completas y comprensibles). El formato es limpio y en buen orden. Se dirige a la audiencia apropiada.
ACEPTABLE	En general, las matemáticas son cuidadosas y exactas, pero existen pocos errores en el trabajo o en la lógica aplicada. Consideró un número limitado de variaciones posibles. Solamente se usa una representación. Es posible que el análisis necesita más cuidado.	Es posible que necesita mejorar la organización. Todo el trabajo está completo. Puede ser que las recomendaciones no están relacionadas completamente a los resultados o a los descubrimientos. Es posible que le falta generalizaciones y predicciones o preguntas adicionales.	En general el lenguaje es claro y completo. El trabajo es exacto y limpio. Es posible que la audiencia no está identificada claramente. Puede ser que las fuentes de información no están completas.
LISTO PARA REVISIÓN	El trabajo puede ser el comienzo de un reporte aceptable, pero las matemáticas necesitan una revisión cuidadosa y correcciones o refino.	Debe r ectificar, como necesario, los procesos usados. Preguntas de foco del maestro le ayudará con las revisiones.	El reporte provee un comienzo pero necesita revisiones importantes.
VOLVER A EMPEZAR/ ENSEÑAR DE NUEVO	La calidad de trabajo necesita mejoramiento o el tópico no es útil. Necesita volver a empezar el proyecto con más instrucciones.	Se necesita más instrucción para encontrar los procesos que trabajarán en ésta investigación.	El reporte necesita más dirección en aplicando el formato, lenguaje, u otros criterios.

■ ASSESSMENT

Assessment Alternatives
Jean Stenmark

EQUALS Programs
Lawrence Hall of Science,
1 Centennial Drive, U.C. Berkeley,
Berkeley, CA 94720-5200
510-642-1823

$4.00

Mathematics Assessment
Jean Stenmark

NCTM
1906 Association Drive
Reston, VA 22091
800-235-7566

$8.50

NCTM 1993 Yearbook - Assessment
Norman L. Webb, Aurthur F. Coxford

NCTM
1906 Association Drive
Reston, VA 22091
800-235-7566

$20.00

Measuring Up

Math Sciences Education Board
2101 Constitution Ave, NW
Washington DC 20418
202-334-3313

$10.95

■ GROUP WORK/ COLLABORATIVE WORK

Cooperative Learning
Spencer Kagan, Ph.D

Resources for Teachers
27134 Paseo Espada #202
San Juan Capistrano, CA 92675
714-248-7757

$25.00

Cooperative Learning in Mathematics
Neil Davidson

Addison-Wesley Publications,
Supply Division
Route 128, Reading, MA 01867
800-624-0822

$32.00

Math Talk
Mathematical Association (UK)

Heinemann
361 Hanover Street,
Portsmouth, NH 03801-3959
603-431-7894

$12.50

■ CURRICULUM RESOURCES: GENERAL

AIMS, Activities and Newsletter

AIMS
P.O. Box 7766,
Fresno, CA 93727
209-255-4094

$25/yr

The Book of Think
Marilyn Burns

Little Brown and Company
200 West Street,
Waltham, MA 02154
800-343-9204

$9.70

Books You Can Count on, Linking Mathematics and Literature
Rachel Griffiths and Margaret Clyne

Heinemann
361 Hanover Street,
Portsmouth, NH 03801-3959
603-431-7894

$13.50

Problem of the Week
L. Fisher and B. Medigovich

Dale Seymour Publications
P.O. Box 10888,
Palo Alto, CA 94303-0879
800-872-1100

$16.00

Writing to Learn Mathematics
Joan Countryman

Heinemann
361 Hanover Street,
Portsmouth, NH 03801-3959
603-431-7894

$12.50

■ CURRICULUM RESOURCES

A Collection of Math Lessons (Grades 6-8)
Marilyn Burns

The Math Solution Publications
(distributed by Cuisenaire)
P.O. Box 5026,
White Plains, NY 10602-5026
800-237-3142

$14.95

Data Sense

Glencoe Division, Macmillan/McGraw-Hill
936 Eastwind Drive
Westerville, OH 43081
614-890-1111

Designing Spaces

Educational Development Center
55 Chapel Street
Newton, MA
617-969-7100

Middle Grades Math Project

Addison-Wesley
Route 128,
Reading, MA 01867
800-447-2226

■ SUPPORT DOCUMENTS

Dealing with Data and Chance (grades 5-8)

NCTM
1906 Association Drive,
Reston, VA 22091-1593
800-235-7566

$15.00

Developing Number Sense in the Middle Grades (grades 5-8)

NCTM
1906 Association Drive,
Reston, VA 22091-1593
800-235-7566

$10.50

Geometry in the Middle Grades (grades 5-8)

NCTM
1906 Association Drive,
Reston, VA 22091-1593
800-235-7566

$15.00

Mathematics Framework for California Public Schools, K-12 (1991)

CA State Dept. of Ed.
Bureau of Publications - Sales
P.O. Box 271,
Sacramento, CA 95802-0271
916-455-1260

$5.50

Mathematics Teaching in the Middle Grades - Journal

NCTM
1906 Association Drive,
Reston, VA 22091-1593
800-255-9566

$40/yr.

Measurement in the Middle Grades (grades 5-8)

NCTM
1906 Association Drive,
Reston, VA 22091-1593
800-235-7566

$12.00

NCTM Curriculum and Evaluation Standards For School Mathematics

NCTM
1906 Association Drive,
Reston, VA 22091
800-235-7566

$25.00

NCTM Professional Standards for Teaching Mathematics (1991)

NCTM
1906 Association Drive,
Reston, VA 22091
800-235-7566

$25.00

Patterns and Functions (grades 5-8)

NCTM
1906 Association Drive,
Reston, VA 22091-1593
800-235-7566

$13.00

■ EQUITY

Breaking the Barriers: Helping Female and Minority Students Succeed in Mathematics Beatriz Chu Clewell, Bernice Anderson, Margaret Thorpe

Jossey-Bass
350 Samsone Street,
San Francisco, CA 94101
415-433-1767

$29.95

Everybody Counts Lynn Steen

Mathematical Sciences Education Board Publications
2101 Constitution Avenue NW,
Washington, DC 20418
800-624-6242

$8.00

How Schools Shortchange Girls The AAUW Report, 1992

American Association of University Women Educational Foundation
1111 16th Street NW,
Washington, DC 20036-4873
800-424-9717

$16.95